THE HAUNTING OF VIRGINIA'S STATE CAPITOL COMPLEX

L ///POLICING THE PARANORMAL/// PO

Best Wishes!

Paul

True Stories of Police Officers' Encounters with the Supernatural

Paul Hope

4880 Lower Valley Road • Atglen, PA 19310

Published by Schiffer Publishing, Ltd.
4880 Lower Valley Road
Atglen, PA 19310
Phone: (610) 593-1777; Fax: (610) 593-2002
E-mail: Info@schifferbooks.com.

For the largest selection of fine reference books on this and related subjects,
please visit our website at
www.schifferbooks.com.
You may also write for a free catalog.

This book may be purchased from the publisher.
Please try your bookstore first.

We are always looking for people to write books on new and related subjects. If you
have an idea for a book, please contact us at
proposals@schifferbooks.com.

Schiffer Books are available at special discounts for bulk purchases for sales promotions or
premiums. Special editions, including personalized covers, corporate imprints, and excerpts can
be created in large quantities for special needs. For more information contact the publisher.

Designed by RoS
Type set in SquareSlab711 Bd BT/NewBskvll BT

ISBN: 978-0-7643-4320-9
Printed in The United States of America

text and images by author
unless otherwise stated

"THE EYE SEES ONLY WHAT THE MIND IS PREPARED TO COMPREHEND."

—*Henri Bergson*
19th Century French Philosopher

Acknowledgments

First, I'd like to mention that although this book has my name on the cover, it is the product of many people who provided me with the material, motivation, and inspiration to fill the chapters.

While writing this book, I entered into collaboration with a wide range of people who freely offered their experiences in order to shed light on some of the strange, and often profound, events that haunt the State Capitol and the surrounding area. And for their effort, patience, and understanding, I am forever thankful.

Foremost, I extend my appreciation to the Virginia Division of Capitol Police for not only providing me with the opportunity to serve with one of the finest law enforcement agencies in the Commonwealth, but also for granting the support I so greatly needed in order for this book's concept to become a reality. To all the witnesses of the paranormal whose names appear within these pages, I so greatly appreciate your cooperation, for without your unwavering support for the project and your honest and in-depth testimonials, there simply would be little of interest to fill the pages.

In particular, I would like to thank Assistant Chief of Police (Ret.) Mike Jones for his generous Foreword, and all the past and present members of the Division of Capitol Police who directly contributed; Chief Kimberly S. Lettner (Ret.), Captain Randy Howard, Phil White, Brian Alexander, Brian Loving, Mike Fiedler, John Wilde, Ken (surname withheld), Jose DeJesus, Jerry Chandler, Kenny Perry, John McKee, Steve Robinson, Mike Walter, Robert Toms, John Nicholson, John Fabian, and Emma (you know who you are).

I'd also like to extend my wholehearted appreciation to others who contributed their chilling tales and otherworldly experiences, including Tutti and Maria at the Mansion, George Mitchell, Julia Callow, and Edward Chase.

Of course, my greatest appreciation goes to my wife, Lisa, who provided constructive feedback, encouragement, and support during the writing of this tome. To Julie Fabian, who spent many long hours proofreading the manuscript and offering great advice. Also, to my sister Jennifer, who so graciously provided me with the photo of the Douglas Head. And, of course, to my mom, Elaine, and Dad, Allen, who not only provided the spine-tingling details of their ghostly experiences at the Douglas Head Hotel, but ignited my initial interest in the paranormal back when I was just a child with their regular accounts of the ghost they simply referred to as *The White Lady*. Thanks Mom and Dad. Finally, all those childhood sleepless nights spent hiding beneath my comforter, convinced that *The White Lady* had followed us home from the hotel have paid off!

Thank you all! It has truly been an adventure.

Dedication

For my wife, Lisa, for supporting me through this arduous project. And to the men and women of the Virginia Division of Capitol Police, past and present, who have made the department one of the finest law enforcement agencies in the Commonwealth of Virginia.

Thank you!

Contents

Foreword

—Major Michael A. Jones (Retired)

Assistant Chief of Police

Virginia Capitol Police

The Capitol Square of Virginia is hallowed ground—full of history. The home of the oldest legislative body in the New World and of the governor of Virginia shares Capitol Square with leaders, legends, losers, heroes, philosophers, and everyday folk. It is a special place, one that has witnessed the creation of history since our country began. It is an old place...and like so many other old places, it is populated with the trappings of the spirits of those who have gone before us. Tragedy and triumph, victory and defeat, pain and pleasure, life and death, all share a place in time in Capitol Square. In my time, we endured the uncertainty of Y2K, the terror of 9-11, the uncertainty of anthrax scares, the violence of the Sniper, the intensity of violent demonstrations, the random violence of an urban city, the fear of pandemic influenza, in addition to the day-to-day rhythms of maintaining order in a disorderly world. Many things happened here, including violent death.

Having been privileged, for a time, to lead the nation's oldest police force—the Virginia Capitol Police—we have been witnesses to the interplay of life on Capitol Square. Along with the antics of the human world, many officers, including myself, have been witnesses to things that just could not be explained. Police officers are natural born skeptics: show us proof. However, on cold, quiet nights, many of us were witnesses to things that had no proof: no fingerprints, DNA, or trace evidence. I can vouch for the veracity of the witnesses whose stories appear in this book. I know their minds...and I know their hearts. They were reluctant to tell their stories, as many of them could not believe what they themselves experienced.

So gentle reader, I encourage you to open your mind and go on patrol with my officers...and listen as you walk through this hallowed place for the things yet to be seen and heard...

Wait a minute...What was that?

Introduction

"Ghost." What does the word mean to you? Spirit, Demon, Poltergeist? They are all words that conjure up images of terror limited only by our imaginations, and influenced largely by popular, modern movie culture. But to me, tales of ghosts and hauntings were as much a part of the reality of my childhood in the Isle of Man, where I grew up, as were other common local myths and legends. Superstitions run deep there and its long history is rich with ghostly tales that lead to the island being considered as one of the most haunted places in the British Isles.

Most people do not have any idea where the Isle of Man is. In fact, I have met few people outside of the British Isles who know anything about the island, but I feel very lucky to have grown up there and to have experienced the culture and traditions firsthand. Stories of ghosts and legends are an integral part of Manx folklore and I believe that most Manx people are proud of the supernatural element of their heritage.

Located in the middle of the Irish Sea, approximately equidistant from England to its east and Ireland to its west, the Isle of Man has its roots set deep in Celtic history. In fact, Viking burial grounds and primordial settlements abound throughout the island and ancient castles and herring-towers dot the coastline, giving rise to the mystical atmosphere that has supported myth, legend, and folklore for centuries throughout the Celtic nations.

It is on this island that, at an early age, I had my first experiences with the supernatural. These experiences led me to develop a lifelong fascination with the paranormal, not as a die-hard believer, but as a person who accepted that there quite possibly could exist a realm way beyond the limits of our own rationale, and that maybe supernatural forces are at work in this world, not meaning us harm, but merely coexisting and occasionally interacting with us. What began for me as a general curiosity in the topic later developed into an avid interest that I retained long after leaving the Isle of Man for the United States. And even though I am now far from the superstitious influences of the Manx culture, it seems that I continue to unintentionally cross paths with the paranormal.

Although throughout my life I have experienced the unearthly on several occasions during my everyday normal activities, it was while working as a police officer that I had many of my most interesting experiences. In what I, and many others like me, have come to consider most likely one of the most haunted places in the United States, I had the unique opportunity to experience the paranormal firsthand, while also learning of similar supernatural occurrences regularly experienced by fellow police officers and state employees.

Surprisingly, through my own research, I learned that although there are numerous books available that list hundreds of haunted places and ghost stories involving Virginia, none have focused on the State Capitol. With so many stories of frequent and often frightening paranormal activities in and around the State Capitol grounds, I can only conclude that the witnesses to these paranormal events were less than willing to share their stories outside of law enforcement or other professional circles, as was I. But fortunately, I had the unique opportunity to serve for a few years as a member of Virginia's Division of Capitol Police. It was while serving as a Virginia Capitol Police Officer that I had several encounters with the paranormal, incidents that refueled my fascination with the supernatural and led to my being privy to numerous accounts of ghostly goings-on from my coworkers. It is these accounts and personal experiences that I wish to share with you.

I don't expect to convince non-believers of the existence of ghosts within the grounds of Virginia's Capitol and its surrounding buildings with the events detailed here. And I am not a self-proclaimed paranormal investigator, psychic medium, sensitive, or any other form of *ghost hunter* (although I do have the utmost respect for those who are). I am only a veteran police officer with a curiosity-fueled interest in the paranormal. My only intention is to provide others who are interested in the supernatural with an insight into the paranormal activities occurring in and around the Capitol grounds, in the words of those who experienced the events and whose credibility is held to the highest standards, as peace officers assigned to protect our state seat of government. I also honestly believe that what is considered the epicenter of Virginia politics may also be an epicenter of paranormal activity.

On the subject of personal paranormal experiences, I believe it's important to shed some light on the experience itself. I know it's strange to say, but most people I have ever talked to about their ghostly encounters have tried to convey the acute sensation they have felt when in the presence of the paranormal. I will try to convey that same sensation, which some may call the sixth sense, but I find that words cannot accurately describe it. The feeling is unlike any other sensation, and it reinforces the fact that what you are experiencing is indeed paranormal. I have spoken to many people who swear that even the first time they witnessed strange phenomena, this intense sense of feeling convinced them that what they were experiencing had no rational explanation. The feeling of a strange heaviness of the air, a tingling of the spine, an occasional smell of something alien to the environment, heightened audible and visual senses, and the overwhelming sensation that you are not alone when all other conventional wisdom indicates that you are, all create the strange but unmistakable aura. And, coupled with either a sudden acute sense of dread or fear, once experienced, it's a feeling a person never forgets, and after witnessing multiple paranormal events, even learns to trust.

It's this so-called sixth sense, and not the assistance of modern ghost-hunting equipment, such as Electromagnetic Field (EMF) detectors, electronic audio recorders, and infra-red cameras (all commonly utilized by ghost hunters and paranormal investigators), that I have learned to trust and rely on when faced with ghostly encounters. But, although my senses leave me with little doubt of what I have experienced, I still always make a conscious effort to find a rational explanation for strange events and not just automatically assume that such events are paranormal in nature.

So please, as you read on, don't just assume that I, or anyone else featured, jumped to conclusions when faced with personal experiences of unexplained phenomena without first looking for rational explanations. I, like many of my colleagues, always search for the logical explanation. But sometimes, a person's senses can convince them that what they are experiencing is nothing other than paranormal. Personally, after exhausting all other possible theories, I've learned to trust my instincts and accept that there may be other forces at work in this world that are well beyond conventional understanding, things that exist around us, but remain unseen until they unexpectedly make their presences known.

Another element I feel that readers should be aware of is the different types of paranormal activity that are alleged to occur. Experts have classified different characteristics of a haunting into several distinct theories, two of which are the *residual haunting* and the *intelligent haunting*. The theory of residual haunting suggests that sudden traumatic or emotional events, such as untimely, painful, or tragic deaths, may leave an imprint of emotional energy within the surrounding environment where the events occurred. These imprints may have the ability to replay themselves, under certain conditions and circumstances, as if the environment itself is reliving a distant memory. This theory may explain such haunting characteristics as phantom footsteps and wandering apparitions, and even such alleged sights and sounds, for example, as past Civil War battles said to have been witnessed replaying themselves on historic battlefields, such as in Gettysburg, Pennsylvania.

But, what if the characteristics of a haunting show signs of intelligent communication? Surely this can't be just a celestial recording of a past event, somehow trapped within its environment, being replayed like an otherworldly movie. These haunting characteristics, such as disembodied voices that appear to respond intelligently to human questions, poltergeist activity (the phenomena of objects moved by unseen and unexplained forces) that centers around certain people, and other seemingly focused ghostly behavior, all appear to be an entity's attempt at intelligent interaction with its living audience, and so differentiates it from the theory of being residual.

Like I mentioned before, I am not an expert on the paranormal, nor do I pretend to be, but I have been fortunate enough to gain a personal insight into the activities of hauntings, both residual and intelligent. There are a wide variety of alleged paranormal activities detailed within this book, witnessed by myself and others, which provoke the question of the existence of life after death. Is there another realm of existence after departing this world? I can't say for sure. But the testimony of my friends and colleagues, and the hundreds of stories I have read and heard from people all over the world who believe they have experienced ghostly events, definitely supports this theory.

Whatever you believe, however, try to keep an open mind as I entertain you with my personal experiences with the paranormal, dating back to my childhood, and the later experiences of myself and others in and around the Virginia State Capitol. Each story is written from personal testimony, related to me during many long and detailed interviews with people who only wish to share their strange and exciting experiences with those who are interested. And before you question my credibility or the credibility of those who graciously provided me with details of their own paranormal experiences, I must tell you that while working as an officer of our nation's oldest and proudest police department, I spent three years on the midnight (graveyard) shift, most of which was spent locked alone inside a historic building for eight hours with only a book or magazine, camera monitors, and an endless supply of coffee to keep me company. I had unprecedented access to areas of the Capitol Building, Executive Mansion, State Supreme Court, and several other state buildings on a nightly basis, and have probably walked hundreds of miles within their dark rooms, hallways, and corridors between the hours of midnight and 8 a.m. So, I believe that if anyone is in a position to unintentionally happen upon paranormal activity in any of the reportedly haunted properties within the Capitol Complex, it is a Capitol police officer patrolling the grounds and buildings during the midnight shift. It is these officers, as well as several other state employees who work within these buildings, who have unselfishly come forward to share in detail their ghostly experiences in order to provide others with a thrilling insight into what really goes on in and around our state's Capitol when the sun goes down and the lights go out.

So, sit back, open your mind, read, and enjoy, as I detail a long and exciting list of intriguing paranormal events. And please, feel free to visit Virginia's historic seat of government and see the hauntings for yourself. Even if you wish to only visit Virginia's Capitol to view its celebrated sights and architectural splendor, do so with an open mind. And who knows, you may even be fortunate enough to catch a glimpse of the paranormal yourself; stranger things have happened!

AUTHOR'S NOTE: Some of the names of witnesses featured in this book have been changed at their request, but the majority of people interviewed gave their express permission to use their real names, adding another element of credibility to the many exciting personal accounts featured.

Part One

AUTHOR EXPERIENCES

Chapter 1

A Childhood Introduction to the Paranormal

Growing up in the Isle of Man, I often heard tales of ghosts, witches, and similar legends. The island is full of supernatural folklore and lays claim to numerous paranormal entities, including its own colony of fairies; a ghostly black dog called the *Moddy-Dhoo*, that is said to haunt the ancient ruins of Peel Castle on the west coast of the island; and the *Buggane*, a mythical demon that allegedly is responsible for the violent destruction of the roof of St. Trinian's Church in retaliation for the constant ringing of the church's bells.

As a child, I quite regularly heard these stories, recited by friends and family, or even school teachers, especially around Halloween—another prominent Manx-Celtic tradition known locally as *Hop-Tu-Naa*. Even my grandmother often told the story of a ghost that visited her and my grandfather shortly after they were first married, as they both lay in bed late one night. My grandmother awoke to the sight of a ghostly apparition of a woman staring at them from the foot of the bed. After waking my grandfather, they both observed the apparition leave the foot of the bed and exit the room through a locked door.

The ancient ruins of Peel Castle, Isle of Man, host many a ghostly legend, including that of the Moddy-Dhoo. *Photo by author*

These tales were not intended to terrify, but were merely meant to entertain as an integral part of our culture and heritage. The Manx, as natives of the Isle of Man are known, tend to be very superstitious people and most maintain a healthy respect for the supernatural. So, it is of no surprise that my parents often told my siblings and me, while we were very young, of a ghost that they and several other people had become accustomed to witnessing at a majestic cliff-top hotel where they both once worked.

The Haunted Hotel

The Douglas Head Hotel has stood proudly atop the 200-foot cliffs overlooking the Douglas Bay, the island's main harbor, since 1869. It has been the source of entertainment for thousands of British tourists who, for decades, visited the island in search of its magnificent views, sandy beaches, and of course the legendary motorcycle TT Races.

Similar in appearance to a castle, the hotel was built around a herring-tower, a sixty-foot stone tower that predates the first lighthouses and was intended as a navigational aid for ships approaching the harbor. The tower overlooked the hotel's three stories of guestrooms, bars, and dance halls, and still stands to this day, although the hotel has since been demolished and replaced with luxury apartments.

During its heyday, in the late 1970s and early 1980s, the hotel provided a popular entertainment night spot for seasonal tourists, while also offering a source of employment for many locals, including both my parents. Throughout the long summer season, while our mother worked, my older brother and sister and I would spend our days at the hotel, exploring the fortress-like location and its acres of surrounding property that led down to a secluded rocky cove, the outer harbor, and the picturesque Douglas Head Lighthouse.

It was while working long hours and late nights during several summer seasons at the location that my mother recalls herself and numerous others experiencing the ghostly presence of a woman dressed in gray roaming the hotel's rooms and corridors adjacent to the tower.

Perched high above the entrance to the island's main harbor, the former Douglas Head Hotel, now apartments, still retains its classic look. The Herring tower remains to this day, overlooking the center of the building, and may still host the location's ghostly inhabitant. *Photo Courtesy of Jennifer Hope*

On one such occasion, while working alone in one of the lounge rooms, my mother observed a metal ashtray slide noisily for several feet across a barroom table, before crashing to the floor, as if propelled by unseen hands. She often told me and my siblings of other encounters with the ghost that included regular observations of the phantom's poltergeist-like behaviors. These activities even included the moving of chairs that had been placed upon tables by the staff. The chairs would be set on top of the furniture to enable the cleaning of the carpet beneath, but some of the chairs would be mysteriously returned to their upright positions beneath the tables before the employees had finished positioning the remaining chairs in the room.

17

The ghost's disembodied voice was also heard several times calling my mom's name, as if to get her attention, and once she was even tapped on the shoulder from behind, startling her and causing her to scream.

One curious patron witnessed the ghostly apparition as he explored the old herring-tower. After descending the stairs and exiting through the door that led to an adjoining room, the patron clearly observed the ghost standing in the doorway. Not realizing the apparition was in fact a ghost, he excused himself and informed her that she would have to move out of the way of the tower door so that he could close it. The ghostly figure then faded gradually and disappeared before his very eyes, at which point he fled in terror.

Although some people associated with the hotel chose to remain skeptical of the ghostly activity, many did admit to witnessing the same female apparition on several occasions, always similarly describing it. The ghost made such a regular appearance around the hotel that the employees, the manager, and his family, and even my older brother, David, became quite used to witnessing the unexplained phenomena occurring within the premises. TV channel dials on the old black and white televisions would be turned by unseen hands, doors would open and close on their own, disembodied footsteps and voices would be heard throughout the hotel, objects would be moved, and even the manager's young daughter recalled a frightful encounter with the ghost on a stairway leading to the second floor of the hotel.

With so much alleged paranormal activity and so many witnesses reporting the same apparition, it was difficult to discount the presence of a paranormal entity in this case. As a teenager, long after the hotel had permanently closed its doors, I would often visit the location and experience a feeling of chills, as I recalled the many stories of ghostly encounters said to have occurred within its castellated walls. Though the building stood empty, I would still attempt to peek through its dark, lifeless windows, hoping to catch a glimpse of a shadowy figure roaming the floors. Alas, I was never fortunate enough to witness the ghost that many before me claimed to have seen. Still, although I never saw it, I feel that I experienced its presence, as the tales of the ghost's haunting remain to this day a prominent part of my childhood memories of the Douglas Head Hotel.

The Ghostly Nun

Another ghost story that always intrigued me as a child was the story of a ghostly lady that allegedly haunted some local property that, centuries before, was home to a nunnery. I quite often heard stories of encounters with the ghost by people who had wandered the public right-of-way that cut through the location, providing a short-cut to the main harbor area.

Usually, those who witnessed the apparition claimed that as they walked beneath the thick canopy of trees that enveloped the right-of-way, following the path of the river and crossing beneath a steam-railway bridge, they encountered the apparition of a misty female figure watching them from either beneath the trees or above the bridge. It was said by many that the apparition was that of a nun who had perished on the grounds during its tenure as a nunnery.

I never personally crossed paths with this ghostly entity, but I have often walked that same right-of-way and experienced a chilling sensation. What I now find more intriguing about the story is that although the existence of the ghost was never officially verified, as most aren't, a story did appear in the Isle of Man newspapers on the of June 6, 2009, that detailed a recent discovery by archeologists of an unmarked grave containing the remains of a nun. The remains date back several hundred years and were discovered in an area of the property associated with the former nunnery. Coincidence?

Haunted Lane

Another memorable incident that, as a child, fueled my curiosity for the paranormal occurred when I was approximately 9 or 10 years old. At the time, my older, teenage sister had a friend, Julia, who lived with her parents in an old farmhouse set on a large property that accommodated several old stone barns and horse-stables. Nearby this property, in adjoining fields, lay the sparse remains of what were believed to have once been the homes of the families who had tended the surrounding fields centuries before. The long driveway leading to the property was a narrow tree-lined dirt farm-lane surrounded on both sides by open fields and a couple of houses; it stretched for approximately a half-mile before meeting the main road that served the neighborhood where I grew up. At the entrance to the lane was a sign affixed to a tree that read "Private," so it became known to us local kids simply as *The Private Lane.*

Julia drove up and down this lonely, unlit farm-lane during many dark winter evenings as she traveled to and from visiting my sister at our house. And it was on one such dark, winter evening that she had an experience she would never forget—an experience that caused her to arrive at our house crying, visibly panic-stricken, and unwilling to travel that farm-lane alone for weeks after.

After being calmed by my mom, Julia recalled how she had been driving down the long, dark lane that evening in her little Mini Cooper, when suddenly she heard a loud thud from the front of her vehicle. Fearing that she had accidentally struck an animal or maybe even damaged her car, Julia stopped her vehicle, stepped out, and walked around to the front of the car expecting to see damage or possibly an injured animal of some sort. As she stood in the beam of her car's headlights, looking around the front of the vehicle, she was suddenly overcome with an intense sense of fear and the unmistakable feeling that someone was standing right next her. Startled, Julia turned to get back in her car, and as she did, she noticed a tall, dark, shadowy figure standing right next her. Although terrified by the ordeal, Julia was later able to describe the apparition as taking the familiar form of a person, but lacking the features of a living person, and instead, appearing as more of a solid three-dimensional shadow.

After momentarily standing frozen with fear at the sight of the apparition, Julia managed to jump into her car and race to our house, where she recalled what she had just witnessed. She was so traumatized by the event that my mom had to call Julia's dad to collect her and take her home, as she was unwilling to make the short journey alone.

A few days later, Julia again described the events of that evening and also informed us of several strange events that had previously taken place on the property where she lived that were witnessed by her and her parents. She recalled that her two German-Shepherd dogs that guarded the property had on several occasions appeared to become unexplainably upset and confused and had barked repeatedly while appearing to focus their attention on unseen things in the dark. Her horses would also become upset in the middle of the night, making noise and stomping around inside the stable for no apparent reason.

Then there was the unexplained humming noise, like that of a person faintly humming a tune that could often be heard late at night emanating from a recently renovated section of the old house. Of course, Julia and her parents searched for obvious explanations before assuming the presence of the paranormal, but regardless of their preference for rational thought, they could not ignore the fact that the home seemed to possess a distinctly uncomfortable atmosphere that made one consider the possibility that the location was indeed haunted.

My friends and I had been to the property where Julia lived several times, and would play in the fields surrounding her residence quite regularly. But, when the sun went down, we considered the area pretty much off limits. Not because there were no street lights, but because during the nighttime hours there was definitely an eerie feeling that descended on the fields.

In fact, I can remember one evening in particular when a couple of my friends and I had decided to ride our bicycles up to the top end of the lane. It was late one summer evening and the sun was beginning to disappear beyond the horizon as we made our way up the dirt track beneath the shadow of the tall trees.

Due to the lane's steadily increasing gradient, about half-way up, we decided to push our bikes instead of riding them. We were walking and chatting away as we approached the upper end of the lane and noticed that it was now beginning to get quite dark. Looking back down the long narrow lane, it appeared like an endless dark tunnel formed by the shadows of the thick overhanging trees, and I hoped it wouldn't be too dark to safely navigate my way around the many pot-holes and ruts that dotted the track's uneven surface.

I can clearly remember approaching the last hundred yards or so at the top of the lane, far beyond the place where Julia had experienced her frightening ordeal and I could see the distant lights of her house through the darkness. Suddenly, I was overcome with the strange feeling that something bad was about to happen. It was a weird feeling that I was completely unfamiliar with and it made me feel extremely uncomfortable. My two friends had also stopped and it appeared that none of us were willing to continue any further up the lane. We couldn't see anything in the dense shadows of the trees, but there was a definite eerieness about the place. Goosebumps and a subtle sense of fear set in and I remember all three of us, without saying a word, hopping on our bicycles and pedaling as fast as we could towards the bottom end of the lane and the comfort of the street lights.

I realize that most people would consider this experience as simply the product of the imagination of a scared child. But, I assure you, I will never forget the feeling I experienced in the darkness at the top of that lane—a feeling that prevented me from ever returning to the location during the evening hours. I have since only experienced it when faced with the presence of the paranormal, leading me to consider that whatever may have been lurking at the top of that lane was quite possibly supernatural.

Maybe the presence was the same shadow person that frightened Julia as she drove down the lane. Maybe the fields surrounding the top of the lane are in fact haunted by the spirits of those who once lived on the land. Who knows? All I know is that at the top of that dark lane, I first experienced a sensation that I have come to trust as a reliable indicator of the presence of the paranormal, a feeling like no other and a feeling that leaves little doubt in my mind that the dead may sometimes return, for whatever reason, and that they possess the ability to interact with the living. The living need only maintain an open mind to the possibility that not everything is as black and white as logic would lead us to believe, and there in fact exists a large gray area where the laws of science become blurred and passed souls are said to wander.

It is experiences and stories like these, as well as numerous other local legends and folklore, that first sparked my early childhood interest in the supernatural. But I had no idea that what began as a mild curiosity in the subject would develop into a lifetime fascination, as I experienced my own chance encounters with the paranormal—chance encounters that began in the Isle of Man and continued to occur even after I crossed the Atlantic Ocean and made my new home in the USA, far away from the superstitious influences of my homeland.

Chapter 2

Early Personal Experiences with the Paranormal

It was several years after the previously described events that I had what I believe to be my first up-close encounter with the supernatural. At the time, I was working as a personal trainer at a local fitness center called The Nautilus, located in the Isle of Man's capital town of Douglas and situated above a popular clothing store in the busy town center. The building that housed The Nautilus was a four-story, red-brick structure that had been standing for several decades on a busy stretch of the main shopping district called Strand Street. Located on the second floor of the building, the fitness facility was accessed through a narrow entrance-way and steep staircase that led above the first floor clothing store to the upper levels. I had been working at the facility for several months before I began noticing weird things happening and often felt I was not alone when there was no other person in the building.

On a couple of occasions, while alone in the gym around closing time, I had been quite startled to hear footsteps and other strange noises, such as knocking and scratching, or what sounded like objects being moved around inside the main gym area. Upon investigating, I never observed anything that would lead me to believe that the premises was haunted and I dismissed the strange noises as just sounds created by the building's aged heating pipes or electrical wiring. That was until I had an unwelcome experience that caused me to believe otherwise.

Not Just a Shadow

Early one morning, I was alone in the men's changing rooms, cleaning the bathrooms and showers in preparation for the start of the business day. The shower room consisted of a small, well-lit, yellowish-colored, ceramic-tiled room with only one door leading out into the main changing-room area. Immediately facing the entrance to the shower room was a single, small toilet cubicle backed by another ceramic-tiled wall. I had been cleaning the room for several minutes, fully aware that the fitness center was not yet open and the front door of the business was locked. I was also fully aware that I was the only person on the second floor of the building.

As I was accustomed to being alone in this area of the building so early in the morning, I was not in the least concerned about experiencing anything out of the ordinary. But, on this particular occasion, I was strangely overcome with the unmistakable feeling that I was being watched. So intense and uncomfortable was the feeling that I stopped what I was doing and called out to see if anyone was there. After receiving no response, I dismissed my instincts and continued spraying down the walls of the shower with the water-hose. As I resumed the task, I continued to become increasingly aware of a strange presence, only now I sensed that there was definitely someone standing directly behind me. At that moment, I was looking out of the shower room and at the back wall of the toilet facing the doorway. The wall was wet from the spraying of the hose and I could clearly see my reflection in the tiles. Only, as well as recognizing my own reflection, I could also clearly see the dark silhouette of another person's shadowy image standing behind me and slightly off to my left. The dark figure appeared several inches taller than me and its head and shoulders were clearly visible in the reflection in the tiles. The hair on the back of my neck was standing straight up and I was momentarily frozen with fear. As I stood there for a second or two, but what seemed like an eternity, I watched as the shadowy figure suddenly moved slowly, but steadily, to my right and disappeared as it crossed out of the view of the doorway. At this point, my fear released its paralyzing grip and I dropped the water-hose and fled the bathroom. I was so scared that I ran through the gym towards the front exit, momentarily stumbling as I entered the reception area, and only managing to regain my composure as I reached the top of the stairs leading to the entrance. It took several long minutes and a strong cup of tea before I was finally able to calm my nerves, and even longer until I could persuade myself to re-enter the changing rooms.

Later that morning, I recalled the incident to my boss, George. I expected him to laugh and tell me I was crazy, but to my surprise, he told me he was shocked I hadn't had any similar experiences in the building previously. A little curious as to this statement, I asked him what he meant, and he responded by telling me that he had also experienced several strange events in the building that he believed were quite possibly paranormal in nature. He recalled a couple of incidents of suspected activity that he had personally witnessed within the building, such as flickering lights, unexplained cold spots, and disembodied footsteps and voices, but one story that truly grabbed my attention was an incident that had involved one of his girlfriends, who he believes unwittingly became the victim of a paranormal entity within the fitness center.

An Unseen Entity

George recalled that on the day of the incident he and his girlfriend had been working in the gym for most of the day. At around ten o'clock that evening, after closing the business, they both decided to take a short walk down the street to one of the local restaurants for a drink and something to eat. As was usual, George brought his dog, Bonzo, an aging overweight Golden Labrador, to the fitness center with him. Bonzo went most places with George, and on this evening, he would be treated to a walk up the street to the restaurant, followed by a period of restrained boredom while leashed to a drain-pipe at the front of the establishment, where he would await George's eventual exit and journey home. Although Bonzo was extremely passive in nature, he did not take kindly to being tied up and left alone outside the restaurant. So, he did what most dogs do when tied up: he barked repeatedly for his owner's attention. Eventually, the manager of the restaurant politely asked George to get rid of the dog.

It was at this point that George's girlfriend realized she had left her purse back at The Nautilus and offered to walk Bonzo the short two blocks back to the fitness center where she would retrieve her purse and secure Bonzo inside the business until she and George had finished their meal. So, George's girlfriend and Bonzo walked the short distance back to the gym, while George remained at the restaurant.

Inside the fitness center, the main switch for all the interior lights was located in a small electrical room behind the reception desk, so the girlfriend had to make her way up two flights of dimly-lit stairs before navigating her way in the dark, down a short hallway, through a door leading into the reception area, and around the reception desk counter to the electrical room. However, as she reached the top of the stairs, with Bonzo on a leash, and entered through the main doors connecting the stairs to the corridor, Bonzo suddenly started acting strangely.

The dog began yelping and whining and pulling back from the leash in an attempt to turn and go back down the stairs. Assuming that Bonzo just didn't want to be left alone in the fitness center without George, the girlfriend pulled him through the doors and down the dark corridor towards the reception area. But, at this point, the girlfriend became inexplicably overwhelmed with a sense of fear and Bonzo's behavior became increasingly erratic. He appeared to be aggressively barking and snarling at something the girlfriend was unable to see in the pitch darkness of the hallway.

He would repeatedly dart forward and away from the leash tethering him to the girlfriend while bearing his teeth, barking, and snarling. He was not being aggressive towards the girl, but instead appeared to be trying to attack someone or something concealed within the darkness before them.

Overcome with fear, and by now sensing that Bonzo was aggressively trying to protect her from some sort of unseen threat, she turned and ran in terror from the fitness center, closely followed by the dog. With fear in her stride, she fled the facility, only stopping at the entrance long enough to lock the door behind her.

Back at the restaurant, George's visibly shaken and upset girlfriend informed him of the incident and that she believed there was someone or something in the fitness center. So George returned to the business to check it out.

After unlocking the doors, making his way in the dark to the electrical room, and turning on all of the lights, George checked the gym for anything unusual. The behavior of his dog had been extremely out of the ordinary, as Bonzo was not at all aggressive, and George was concerned that someone may have broken into the facility. After a thorough check of the fitness center, George was unable to find anything that would indicate a possible intruder. Instead, the unusual behavior of his dog, and the fact that his girlfriend stated to him that she had experienced a weird sense of fear, during the incident, that left her unwilling to ever again be in the fitness center alone, led George to believe that something entirely different was responsible for the incident. George now suspected that what he had previously experienced in the business, of what he felt was a paranormal entity, may have just made its presence known to someone else, including his dog.

The Misty Apparition

A few months after these incidents, I was again working in the fitness center early one morning, only this time I was not alone. I clearly remember that, on this occasion, there were at least a couple of other staff members in the reception/lounge area of the gym. I was in the gym area, tidying up the weights and equipment in preparation for the opening of the business when, I felt that ever-so-familiar feeling that something strange was present. As I glanced towards the bottom corner of the gym, where a short, but wide, corridor provided a secluded workout spot that led to an enclosed tanning room, I noticed what could only be described as a shadow-like, misty apparition taking the form of a person that stood only about three or four feet tall, and moving slowly, as if floating, towards the center of the gym. Being that I was some distance from the apparition, my first assumption was that my eyes were playing tricks on me, or it was a shadow or possibly even smoke, and I began to walk towards it in order to ascertain the source. But, as I got closer, the image began to fade and then simply disappeared before I got within twenty feet of it.

All the lights were on in the gym and I was confident that what I had just observed was not my eyes playing tricks or a shadow caused by the lights. The apparition had clearly been moving when nothing else in the gym had been, and that area of the gym had no exterior windows that would provide the elements necessary to create such shadows. A quick investigation of the immediate area revealed nothing unusual or any evidence of smoke, so, with a lack of any rational explanation for what I had just witnessed, I reluctantly concluded that the apparition was quite possibly related to my previous paranormal experience.

The only thing that concerned me a little more about this event, as opposed to others I had personally experienced within the building, was the fact that this apparition appeared to be a lot shorter than the one that I had witnessed in the shower room. I now wondered whether there was more than one entity responsible for the paranormal activities within the building, or if what I had just witnessed had in fact been only a partial manifestation of the entity that had previously appeared to me. However, since as I was not, and still am not, a paranormal investigator or parapsychologist of any kind, I never investigated or researched the activities or the history of the building to such a degree as to enable me to solve the mystery behind the apparent haunting.

During my three years employed at the fitness center, I had several more experiences that I could only conclude were the activities of the ghostly entity that I and several other people were convinced haunted the building. Other people also reported weird occurrences throughout the center that may or may not be able to be explained rationally. Unfortunately, the several other experiences I had after my initial introduction to the facility's uninvited guest were less memorable and may also be explained rationally. Weird shadows, banging, scratching, knocking, footsteps, voices, and other peculiar incidents became such regular occurrences within the business that, after a while, they failed to impress or warrant further investigation by those who witnessed them. In fact, other employees of the business came to accept the activity as quite normal.

Since the events I witnessed within The Nautilus Fitness Center, I have only had the fortune of experiencing one other place that truly offered such a frequent variety of intense paranormal activity, and that location will be discussed at length in later chapters and I would have to wait until I left my homeland of the Isle of Man for the United States before I would experience this activity—activity that would leave me and several other witnesses shocked and speechless.

The Haunted House

This center of intense paranormal activity was a house that I lived in for a short time, with my first wife, in the town of Bangor, Maine. The house had stood for at least two decades before my mother-in-law and father-in-law at that time had moved in with their daughter and two sons many years before my arrival in the United States. The year 1994 was the first time I visited their home, when I came to the U.S. for a few weeks to marry the American girl whom I had met back in the Isle of Man some time before.

The residence was a modest, two-story, four-bedroom home with a full basement and detached garage, and stood surrounded by similar houses lining both sides of the street. From the outside, the house didn't appear much different than any other on the long narrow street, but on the *inside,* this family residence concealed a ghostly secret that often disturbed those who stayed there for any length of time, and intrigued the family members who called it their home.

The activities that were regularly witnessed in the home were usually limited to the frequent sounds of heavy footsteps running across the floor of the master bedroom, located directly above the living room. The footsteps were so audibly clear that witnesses could actually sense the vibrations of footfalls throughout the house, as they traveled across the bedroom floor and often down the two small flights of stairs that led to the rear of the dining room adjacent to a downstairs bathroom. The foot of the stairs could not be observed from the living room, but it was a brave soul who dared venture to the base of the thickly carpeted stairs to investigate the disembodied footsteps.

It was while visiting the house for several days in 1994 that I first personally experienced the paranormal activity within the home. I had been sitting in the living room with my wife and several members of her family when I heard the unmistakable sound of loud footsteps coming from the room above. Naively, I simply assumed that there was someone walking around upstairs and inquired as to who it was. I was then calmly, and quite nonchalantly, informed by the members of the household that there was no one upstairs—at least, no one living—leaving me a little surprised and disturbed at the prospect of residing in a seemingly haunted house.

As I visited the home more often, I began to take notice of the footsteps and the frequency at which they occurred. I found that the steps were not just limited to nighttime occurrences, but the daytime, as well. To my relief, I also found that the activity never occurred while there was actually someone upstairs in the house, and most people at the house reported experiencing few other significant paranormal activities other than the footsteps.

I realize that houses make strange sounds when they are expanding and contracting as a result of heat, humidity, and other environmental conditions. I also realize that small animals can sometimes get inside the walls of homes and create sounds that can be mistaken for the paranormal. But these sounds were way beyond the settling noises of wooden beams and floors, or animals small enough to move between floor or wallboards. In my opinion, these noises definitely sounded like footsteps being created by something that could not be seen and something with motions similar to that of a child or small adult.

In 1996, after establishing permanent residency in the United States, my then-wife and I lived at the house for several months. During this period of residence in the home, I quite regularly heard the disembodied footsteps, but never while I was upstairs. In fact, my wife and I actually slept in the very room where the footsteps were frequently heard coming *from*.

Other weird and unexplainable activities were experienced while I resided there, though, not just by me, but my wife, too. Things like the bed shaking in the middle of the night. Not violently, but enough to feel it and make you wonder what was causing it. Nothing else in the room would be shaking, just the bed. On another occasion, my wife and I were in the bedroom putting laundry away when the screw-in light bulb in a lamp atop the bedside table popped out of its fitting and landed several feet across the room. Startled by this event, we both examined the bulb and the lamp, but could find no logical reason for the anomaly. Later, I screwed the bulb back into the lamp and discovered (to both our amazement) that it still worked.

Similar activities occurred during the remainder of my residence at the house, but the one that sticks in my mind most vividly is an incident that involved a possible display of anger by "the entity"—a scene that shocked several of us into leaving the house for an entire evening.

This particular incident occurred while several friends and I, including my brother-in-law, Eddie, were sitting around the dining-room table playing cards, laughing, joking, and drinking a few beers.

We had been playing cards for quite a while when the conversation was interrupted by the distinct sound of the phantom footsteps crossing the master-bedroom upstairs. Bemused, the friends inquired as to the sounds of the footsteps and the conversation quickly turned to the topic of the resident ghost. Eddie then decided that this would be the appropriate time to provoke the ghost and began verbally challenging the entity to come and get us.

This verbal harassment continued for several minutes, against my advice, but obviously fueled by the alcohol that had been consumed. Everyone was feeling unusually brave and confident that there would be little or no consequence to challenging the paranormal. Then it happened. First, a couple of us around the table noticed the slight movement and swinging motion of the brass chandelier that was hanging from the ceiling directly above the dining room table. Hardly noticeable at first, the subtle motion slowly increased, causing all of us to stare at it curiously; then after a minute or two, it gradually subsided. Not convinced that the activity of the chandelier was paranormal, we returned to the conversation and the card game, but just as Eddie resumed dealing the cards, we heard a loud cracking sound, followed by the sight of a thick heavy glass ashtray, which had been sitting in the center of the table, suddenly and violently breaking apart, shooting several large chunks of glass across the table. One of the pieces actually hit me in the chest with enough force to leave a small abrasion on my skin beneath my t-shirt.

Everyone in the room was momentarily stunned. Nothing was said for several seconds as we all tried to make sense out of what we had witnessed. The expressions on everyone's faces said it all. We were all convinced that Eddie had indeed succeeded in provoking the ghost, who, in turn, had violently broken the ashtray. It was then that we quickly decided that we would all vacate the house for the remainder of the evening. It had definitely been, to say the least, a sobering experience.

It would be several years before I again crossed paths with the paranormal. During this time, I was in the Army and don't really remember experiencing anything of significance that would indicate paranormal activity. However, it wouldn't be too long until I would again witness events that I would consider paranormal, and this time I would join a long list of witnesses who had experienced the same strange phenomena that I would come to know on a relatively frequent basis.

Part Two

VIRGINIA'S STATE CAPITOL COMPLEX

Chapter 3

The Virginia State Capitol

In early 2001, I left the U.S. Army and was immediately hired by the Virginia Capitol Police Department (now known as the Division of Capitol Police) in Richmond, Virginia. A relatively small, but unique, law enforcement agency, the Virginia Capitol Police Department is the nation's oldest police agency, established in 1618, when it consisted of a small guard force responsible for the protection of the Colonial Governor of Jamestown.

Now evolved into Virginia's premier specialized police department, the 100 or so members of the Virginia Capitol Police are primarily responsible for the safety and security of the state legislature, state employees, and properties belonging to the State of Virginia located

The historic Virginia State Capitol building overlooks the South gardens of the Capitol Square. This epicenter of Virginia politics may also be the epicenter of paranormal activity. *Photo by author*

Author's Note: Although the Capitol is open to the public during normal business hours, security restrictions exist and prior authorization from the Division of Capitol Police would be required before any formal investigation could be conducted within the Capitol grounds or surrounding State Government properties.

The author proudly displayed the uniform-patch of the Virginia Capitol Police for three years as a member of "the graveyard shift." *Photo by author*

in the downtown area of the City of Richmond. Not limited to these functions, the duties of the Capitol Police also include the protection of the Governor and his family, while at the Executive Mansion, their place of residence in Capitol Square; the protection of the Justices belonging to the Supreme Court of Virginia and the Virginia's Lieutenant Governor and Attorney General; and numerous other general and specialized law enforcement duties.

Located in the heart of downtown Richmond, Virginia's Capitol Complex includes the historic Capitol Building, Executive Mansion, General Assembly Building, the Bell Tower, Supreme Court of Virginia, the Old State Library (now known as the Patrick Henry Building), Old City Hall, the Old Finance Building (originally the State Library Building), the Washington Building, the Jefferson Building, and several historic statues and monuments, all surrounding the twelve-acre Capitol Square.

Tens of thousands of tourists from all over the world visit Capitol Square annually and it is considered one of Virginia's main historic attractions. Still serving the seat of government, the Capitol Square complex becomes a hive of activity during the first few months of every year, as the annual General Assembly convenes and our state legislators tend to the important business of managing the Commonwealth.

Constructed to mimic the appearance of an ancient Roman Temple, complete with several large white pillars overlooking the exterior portico, the picturesque Capitol Building has served as Virginia's seat of government since 1788. During its long tenure, the Capitol has witnessed its fair share of historical moments, including its narrow escape from the burning of downtown Richmond at the hands of Confederate troops in 1865. As well as hosting many past U.S. Presidents, the Capitol has also in the past played host to several foreign dignitaries, including The Marquis de Lafeyette (a French General who served with distinction during the American Revolution), British Prime Ministers Winston Churchill and Margaret Thatcher, and even Queen Elizabeth II of England.

In April 1870, during a Virginia Supreme Court of Appeals hearing, the Capitol witnessed its greatest tragedy. In a second-floor room of the building, proceedings were underway involving a dispute concerning the leadership of the City of Richmond. Under the weight of hundreds of people who had gathered in the courtroom to witness the measures, a balcony collapsed and fell to the courtroom floor. This sudden impact caused the entire floor in the courtroom to collapse and fall into the room below, killing 62 people and injuring another 250. In the months following the tragedy, the area of the Capitol Building where the collapse occurred was hastily rebuilt and evidence of the dreadful event was all but erased, although a plaque does remain on the wall of the room, now known as the Old House Chamber, that clearly describes the events of that fateful day and is a chilling reminder of the building's turbulent history.

Today, the Capitol Building continues to play host to gubernatorial inaugurations and the annual convening of the Virginia General Assembly. It remains the epicenter of Virginia politics. Recently, the building has experienced a multi-million dollar renovation and expansion. However, with such a death toll occurring within the walls of the Capitol Building, and coupled with a relative plethora of alleged paranormal activity, it is often wondered if the tragic souls of the victims of the collapse still wander the halls and corridors as the darkness of night descends on the daily closing of the Commonwealth's legislative body.

A Shadow Figure

During my several years of service with the Virginia Capitol Police, I heard many stories of people's encounters with ghostly apparitions or strange events that witnesses could only conclude as being paranormal activity. At first, I dismissed most of the stories as the product of over-active imaginations, due to the frequency and level of activity that was claimed to have been witnessed. But, as I spent more and more time within the walls of the Capitol Building, and other buildings within the Capitol complex, I became more familiar with the weird sights, sounds, and other unexplained phenomena that quite regularly occurred and spooked even the hardened non-believers.

It was only several days after starting work with the Capitol Police that I experienced my first encounter with the building's paranormal residents. I had been assigned to the midnight shift for training and had been instructed to patrol the Capitol Building, checking all offices and rooms, locking all interior and exterior doors, and turning off all non-essential lights. As a rookie officer, I would learn this function of the Capitol Police from a more experienced veteran of the department, Officer Brian Loving.

It was late at night, probably around twelve-thirty or one o'clock, when we began our patrol of the interior of the Capitol Building. The building's historical significance, coupled with its long, white marble and limestone hallways and ancient architecture, provided a degree of interest to an otherwise mundane task. At this early stage of my employment with the Capitol Police, these late night patrols actually provided a sense of exploration, as I had unprecedented access to areas of the Capitol that were otherwise restricted from the general public. The underground tunnels that connected several buildings surrounding the Capitol, and once led several hundred yards down to the banks of Richmond's James River, were one such area of interest that provided a sense of adventure. Other areas included the Senate and House Chambers that hosted Virginia's legislative bodies as they met to vote on proposed legislation during the annual General Assembly, and the Old Senate and House Chambers that are now preserved as part of Virginia's political history and provide a historical point of interest for visitors.

The second floor, known as the Rotunda, is the main area for visitors to the Capitol and offers the previously mentioned areas of historical interest. The originally white décor of the Rotunda (now yellow since the renovations) was offset on both sides by the brown woodwork and blue and red carpeting of the more recent additions of the House and Senate Chambers, while beyond the large wooden doors of the South entrance of the Rotunda lies the ever-prominent South Portico that overlooks the Capitol gardens and once provided a view of the banks of the James River. In the center of the black and white tiled Rotunda stands a life-sized marble statue of George Washington atop a five-foot pedestal. The statue stands directly beneath the building's famous thirty-foot interior dome that is concealed within the roof of the four-story building. The House and Senate Chambers lie at the east and west ends of the main Capitol Building and were constructed long after the original construction of the Capitol when the legislature simply outgrew the building.

Lying directly behind the statue of George Washington is the entrance to the Old House Chamber and scene of the 1870 tragedy. Two tall, heavy wooden doors open to the largest room of the original Capitol where an impressive life-size, bronze statue of General Robert E. Lee appears to stand guard over the chamber's interior. Overlooking the east and west ends of the room are balconies that provide an elevated viewpoint of the entire chamber, and a tall, wooden throne-like chair, reserved for the House Speaker, sits between two tall, thickly draped windows facing the entrance to the room overlooking an encased ceremonial golden mace. Mounted on the south wall, adjacent to the entrance of the room, is a large plaque commemorating the Capitol disaster of 1870, and polished wooden chairs are positioned neatly in rows throughout the room facing the House Speaker's seat. Several other large windows with thick drapes occupy the remaining two exterior walls of the room, while historic portraits and brass plaques appear to adorn most of the remaining wall space. The coved ceiling of the Old House Chamber creates an illusion of being extremely high and completes the already creative architecture of the room.

Officer Brian Loving and I had been checking the doors and offices of the lower first floor and had eventually made our way up

George Washington stands proud in the Capitol's Rotunda, directly in front of the Old House Chamber. The hostess desk was situated to the left of the chamber doors. *Photo by author*

to the second floor. Entering the second-floor Rotunda level from the west stairs, we checked the Old Senate Chamber and offices to our right and the doors to the South Portico, and then made our way to the Old House Chamber. At this time of night, some of the lights of the Rotunda were on, but others weren't, so the entire Rotunda took on a shaded appearance. There were no lights on in the interior of the Old House Chamber during the nighttime, and so to avoid the task of locating the individual light switches, flashlights were used to quickly inspect the interior of the room for anything unusual or out of place.

We entered the dark spacious room and quickly began to scan the interior with our flashlights. The sight of a General Lee staring down from above his pedestal startled me for a second as he was illuminated by our lights. Aside from that, the only other element that contributed to an uneasy feeling about the room was that the interior was inexplicably cold. For some unknown reason, the interior of the room always felt several degrees cooler than the rest of the building. In fact, it remained so cold, that during the summer months, the doors to the Old House Chamber would be intentionally left open at night in order to assist with the cooling of the rest of the Rotunda level.

As Brian and I scanned the interior from just within the entrance to the room, he suggested that I read the plaque commemorating the 1870 tragedy that was mounted on the south wall, adjacent to the main door. Upon his request, I made my way to the plaque and stood directly in front of it. We both stood facing the plaque, only three or four feet away, and began quietly reading. Our flashlights were the only illumination inside the dark room and they created an eerie glow, but as nothing was moving inside the room, everything appeared completely motionless. Up to our left, and visible to my left side as I read the inscription on the plaque, was one of the room's two balconies that provide elevated audience viewing from each end of the room.

As we stood reading, all of a sudden, out of the corner of my left eye, I noticed movement from the balcony. As I turned to investigate the movement, quite startled by its sudden occurrence, I observed in the dim light created by my flashlight, a dark shadow quickly moving several feet to the left of the position where I had first noticed it in the right-hand corner of the gallery. At the same time I noticed the movement, so had Brian. We were now both standing staring at the empty balcony, still dimly illuminated by our flashlights, but there was nothing there and no sign of any movement. What we had both observed seemed to have disappeared as suddenly as it appeared.

Upon later evaluation of the incident, I surmised that while turning my head to look up, I had clearly observed what I believe to be a dark shadow figure, about the size of a person, quickly move several feet, as if walking from the right corner of the balcony, and then disappear. Brian asked me if I, too, had witnessed the strange anomaly, and while standing next to him, still staring at the gallery, I responded that I believed I had indeed just witnessed what he had observed. Brian then described to me what he had seen and right then I knew that my eyes hadn't deceived me. At that point, keenly aware of an icy-cold chill and an accompanying peculiar atmosphere within the room, I was quite confident that both of us had just witnessed paranormal activity. I believe Brian suspected the same as I did, for he had already turned and made a hasty exit from the room.

For a moment, I just stood there, totally intrigued by what I had witnessed. I understand the possibility of my eyes playing tricks on me, but two people witnessing the same thing at the same time suggests that whatever was there was not a figment of my imagination, nor a result of tired eyes. For several seconds, I scanned the room, hoping to see something again, but to my disappointment, whatever had just made its presence known must have been unwilling to entertain us further.

Outside the Old House Chamber, in the Rotunda, I caught up with Brian. He was standing next to the statue of George Washington and had an expression of annoyance on his face. I asked him if he had ever previously experienced anything like that inside the Capitol, and he commented that he hated it when activity like that occurred while he was inside the building. He went on to tell me that he had on several occasions witnessed what he believes to be paranormal events in the Capitol, including other moving shadows within the Old House Chamber, phantom footsteps, strange disembodied voices, and even a moving object. However, at the time, he declined to discuss the events in detail, stating that the experiences made him feel quite uncomfortable at the prospect of checking the building alone, as officers regularly did.

Brian and I continued our patrol of the building, checking the interior of just about every room and office in the Capitol, and walking every foot of its corridors, but we did not, during that particular night, experience any further paranormal activity. Although, as my service with the Capitol Police progressed, I would walk the dark corridors and rooms of the Capitol Building many more times, and would have several more experiences of my own, while also hearing of numerous other mysterious paranormal encounters from other Capitol Police officers.

The Old House Chamber. General Robert E. Lee stands guard to the right. The balcony that played host to the strange shadow person stands overlooking the far end of the room. *Photo by author*

The plaque commemorating the Capitol disaster of 1870 is displayed on the wall of the Old House Chamber beside the entrance doors. *Photo by author*

CAPITOL DISASTER

THIS TABLET WAS ERECTED UNDER AN ACT OF THE GENERAL ASSEMBLY OF VIRGINIA. APPROVED MARCH 16, 1918---TO MARK THE SCENE OF THE CAPITOL DISASTER WHICH OCCURRED ON APRIL 27, 1870, WHEN THE FLOOR OF THE COURT ROOM OF THE SUPREME COURT OF APPEALS WHICH WAS THEN ABOVE THIS HALL FELL, RESULTING IN THE DEATH OF SIXTY-TWO AND THE INJURING OF TWO HUNDRED AND FIFTY-ONE OTHER PERSONS.

THE FALLING OF THE COURT ROOM WAS OCCASIONED BY THE ATTENDANCE OF AN UNUSUAL NUMBER OF PERSONS ASSEMBLED TO HEAR THE DECISION OF THE COURT IN THE CASE OF ELLYSON VS. CAHOON, KNOWN AS THE RICHMOND MAYORALTY CASE. REPORTED IN XIX GRATTAN, PAGE 673.

The Graveyard Shift

After working for the Capitol Police for several months and graduating from the police academy, I was eventually assigned to the midnight shift, otherwise known as the graveyard shift. I soon discovered, though, working at the Capitol during the nighttime hours gave a whole new meaning to the phrase *graveyard shift*.

It wasn't long before another ghostly incident occurred. After only several nights working the graveyard shift, I had another strange experience inside the Capitol Building. While alone, patrolling the interior of the building, I was again in the area of the second floor Rotunda. Again, the lights were dim, and except for the sound of my own footsteps, the building retained an atmosphere of peaceful tranquility. The cleaning crew had long since gone home and the only other person in the building was another Capitol Police officer, standing guard at the west-entrance, while I performed the night's final check of the interior, turning off all non-essential lights, and locking the interior offices' doors.

As I passed through the area that separates the Old Senate Chamber from the office of the Clerk of the House of Delegates, on my way to the doors that opened to the Capitol's South Portico, my attention was drawn to the unmistakable sound of voices emanating from the interior of the Old Senate Chamber. Curious as to the origin of the voices, I stopped and listened for a few seconds. Thinking that the sounds may have come from my police radio that I was carrying on my gun-belt, I lowered its volume and again listened intently for the voices. After a few more seconds of hearing no voices, I turned and began to continue towards the doors of the South Portico, but as I proceeded, I again caught the faint sound of voices. Bemused, I stopped once more and listened intently, and as I listened, I could definitely detect the sound of indistinct voices from within the Old Senate Chamber. The thick wooden doors of the chamber were locked, but as I continued to listen, I could make out the deep, yet somewhat muffled, voices of at least two men talking—too quiet and muffled for me to make out what they were saying, but audible enough to conclude that the voices were quite possibly coming from at least two men inside the room.

Knowing that there was not supposed to be anyone inside the Capitol Building at such a late hour, and curious as to the origin of the voices, I nervously unlocked one of the heavy wooden doors to the chamber and slowly opened it. As I had taken a couple of steps towards the door, the voices had quickly faded, and as I entered the room, there was only silence and the ever-present smell of years of accumulated furniture polish and varnish. The interior of the room was completely dark and I quickly acquired my flashlight from my belt and shone it around. Inside the room were several rows of polished wooden chairs facing two large windows hung with long heavy drapes. Directly in front of these windows was a long, polished wooden table stretching almost the length of the chamber. Another two large, draped windows occupied the wall directly to the left of the doors, and on the other walls, and between the windows, hung several prominent paintings depicting decisive battles of the Civil War and various portraits of historical figures with gold-colored frames. Thick carpeting and brass fittings finished off the original décor of the room where Virginia's legislative Senate once sat.

As I stepped inside the chamber and shone around my flashlight, I immediately noticed that there was absolutely no one inside the room. Everything was still and completely silent, and there was no sign of anything out of the ordinary. I reached for one of the light switches and illuminated the room while I performed a quick check of the entire interior, looking for radios or any other electrical device that could have been responsible for the voices I had definitely heard. Although I realized the origin of the voices may indeed be paranormal, I felt no chills or any sense of fear resulting from what I had just experienced. But, I did feel entirely uncomfortable inside the room, and after completing my check, I quietly exited and locked the door.

Once outside the room, I opened up the doors to the South Portico and checked the steps leading down to the landscaped gardens of Capitol Square and the area around the exterior of the windows of the Old Senate Chamber. There appeared to be no one hanging around and there was no sign of anyone who may have been responsible for the voices. After a couple of minutes of taking in the moonlit view of some of downtown Richmond's high-rise buildings, that now block the once-prime view of the banks of the James River, I re-entered the Capitol Building and continued my check of the interior.

Still curious as to the origin of the voices I had just heard, I entered the office of the Clerk of the House of Delegates (now the Jefferson Room), located directly opposite the Old Senate Chamber. I turned on the lights, and searched the interior of the office for evidence of anything that could have been responsible for the sounds. Again, I could not locate anything, such as radios or other electronic devices that could have been responsible for the noises. But again, I sensed the distinct feeling that I was not alone, a feeling I would become all too familiar with as I continued my service with the Capitol Police.

The remainder of my check of the Capitol Building proved thankfully uneventful. What had begun as a routine patrol of the interior of the premises had possibly become yet another experience with the paranormal. So, curious as to the origins of these events and the possibility that I was not the only officer who may have experienced evidence of the Capitol's unearthly residents, I began to question my colleagues. And, as you might expect, their answers were often very surprising and equally intriguing.

The Old Senate Chamber. Disembodied voices were heard chatting from within its dark and locked interior. *Photo by author*

Phantom Footsteps

Another memorable experience with the supernatural that occurred while I was working at the Capitol came in the form of phantom footsteps, or *disembodied footsteps* as they are known to paranormal experts.

While working alone in the Capitol Building during the long lonely nighttime hours, I would quite often hear strange noises coming from the rooms and corridors inside the building. Most of these noises I would simply dismiss as the heating and air conditioning pipes expanding and compressing due to fluctuations in temperature, or the old building creaking as it warmed or cooled. But, some noises I could not as easily dismiss, and nor could many of my colleagues.

On several occasions, while I was sitting at my assigned post, just inside the west-entrance of the Capitol Building, during the graveyard shift, I clearly heard footsteps coming down the long corridor just outside the office. The office beside the west-entrance was a small, closet-sized room that contained a tall, narrow podium-style desk concealing a chair where the assigned Capitol Police officer sat and screened everyone who came to the west entrance requesting access to the building. Because the chair and desk were recessed inside the small room, the officer had no view of the length of the corridor that stretched from the west entrance to the east entrance, cutting directly through the center of the first floor. The officer's only view was of the outside, through a small wooden-framed window located just inside the room, adjacent to the entrance, where the officers could observe people approaching the door. Things have changed now since the completion of the Capitol's renovation in 2007, but back then, the office was small and cramped, and considered somewhat inappropriate for the purpose it served.

During the night, if any of the Capitol Building's doors or windows were to open, the security system would indicate the movement either audibly or visually. The old security and fire monitoring system was thankfully replaced during the Capitol's recent renovations, but as sensitive as the old system was, it is difficult to fathom how anyone could enter the building without being detected *and* be responsible for the footsteps that several of my colleagues and I most definitely heard.

I first heard the phantom footsteps after being assigned the Capitol west entrance post during one of my regular nights on the graveyard shift. I had been at the post for several hours and expected to be soon relieved for a well-needed coffee-break by one of the other officers. It was likely around three o'clock in the morning when, to my delight, I heard heavy footsteps echoing down the marble floor of the corridor, coming from the east entrance, directly through the center of the building, approaching my location. As the footsteps appeared to get louder as they approached my location, I arose from the chair behind the desk, in anticipation of being relieved by the officer for my coffee-break, and sauntered out into the corridor. Just as I stepped out into the corridor, expecting to see another officer, the footsteps abruptly ceased. There was no one there. At this point, the hair rose on the back of my neck and I noticed that the air around me was chillingly cold. I shivered as I looked directly down the corridor, but I could not see anyone. The sounds of the footsteps had been so clear I could determine that whoever had made them was only a few feet from the entrance to the small office when they had ceased. Given the proximity of the footsteps at the moment I stepped out into the corridor, I could not believe that someone could have moved fast enough to duck out of view before being seen.

The corridor was now deathly quiet. I knew no one could have entered the building without detection and I quickly began to suspect that what I had just experienced was again possibly paranormal. With my back to the tall, green, wooden doors of the west entrance, I shone my flashlight down the dimly lit corridor, but I did not observe anything or anyone moving. My senses were on high alert as the familiar smell of decades of accumulated floor wax engulfed my nostrils, an odor that was ever-present in many of the historic buildings that surround the Capitol. The hairs on the back of my neck were still raised and the air remained chillingly cold as I slowly walked up the long, dim corridor towards the east entrance. Along the way, I shone my flashlight and checked adjoining hallways for signs of activity, but there was absolutely no one there.

It was several more minutes before I was finally relieved for a coffee break by another officer. I didn't tell him what I had just experienced, partly out of fear of being mocked, and partly because I hoped that he would experience the same activity while I was gone. I would eventually discover that many of my colleagues had experienced the same strange activity as I, and some with such frequency that the officers became quite used to its occurrence.

The long main corridor that
runs the length of the first floor
of the Capitol Building, where
phantom footsteps are often
heard wandering throughout
the night. *Photo by author*

The West Entrance of the Virginia State
Capitol building. Directly beyond these
entrance doors, several officers have
witnessed the sound of phantom footsteps
reverberating throughout the main corridor
during the dead of night. *Photo by author*

The Experiences of a Skeptic

Officer Mike Fiedler worked for the Virginia Capitol Police for several years beginning in 2002. Like me, Mike primarily worked the graveyard shift, and also like me, experienced several events of unexplained phenomena within the historic halls and corridors of the Capitol Building.

Mike recently recalled to me that on several occasions, while seated alone late at night at the west entrance of the Capitol Building, he heard the unexplained sounds of voices and footsteps echoing down the main hallway. Of course, upon investigating the sounds, he could never locate anyone or anything that could explain the noises. And, although he never observed anything that could convince him that the Capitol is indeed haunted, Mike did often experience the feeling of cold chills running down his spine as he entered certain rooms within the Capitol or walked its lonely corridors in the middle of the night.

Mike further reiterated to me that he considers himself a skeptic of the paranormal. But, even he admits that the strange events he often witnessed, during many lonely nights patrolling the halls of the Capitol Building, lack any serious rational explanation and may support the claim that the location is indeed haunted.

A Ghostly Interruption

Captain Randy Howard has worked for the Virginia Capitol Police for over twenty years. During that time, he's worked his fair share of graveyard shifts, many of which were spent patrolling the Capitol complex's many historical buildings. So it's of no surprise that with as much experience with the Capitol Police as he has, he, too, has been witness to the location's paranormal activity.

The incident occurred in 1998, while Randy was a sergeant on the graveyard shift. Skeptical of his colleagues' frequent reports of ghostly activity, Randy was not at the least perturbed at the prospect of sitting alone in the dark at the large wooden table, known as the hostess desk, located just outside the tall, wooden doors of the Old House Chamber. The only illumination in the second-floor Rotunda that late at night was a small decorative lamp positioned on a smaller corner table to the rear of the hostess desk, and Randy relaxed in the chair and called his wife on the desk phone.

During his conversation with her, Randy's attention was suddenly drawn to the small lamp as it began flickering erratically. Pausing for a second, Randy turned to observe the lamp behind him as its flickering created an eerie effect in the tranquil darkness of the second-floor Rotunda. But, assuming that there was probably a loose connection or electrical disruption causing the anomaly, Randy turned back around and resumed his phone conversation with his wife. As Randy continued his chat, he was suddenly shocked by the sight of the phone that had been sitting in the middle of the table in front of him, steadily beginning to slide to the right, across the desktop, seemingly propelled by an unseen force.

Mesmerized by what he was witnessing in the flickering light of the Rotunda, Randy continued to observe the phone as it steadily slid to the very edge of the desk before stopping only a couple of inches short of falling to the marble floor. The whole time this unexplained phenomena was occurring, Randy was still grasping the phone's receiver as its coiled cord stretched to its limit as the phone inexplicably scraped across the table's surface.

Seeing the phone stop at the very edge of the desk, and now very conscious of the feeling that he was not quite completely alone within the darkened interior of the Capitol Building, Randy abruptly stated to his wife, "I got to go," and hung up the phone. At this point,

Randy hastily left the second-floor Rotunda area and made his exit from the building.

While talking to Randy about this event, he stated to me that he has never since experienced anything that he considers paranormal within the Capitol complex. In fact, Randy gives the impression that he remains somewhat skeptical of other events allegedly witnessed by others, but he has no doubt as to what he himself witnessed that night in the Capitol, and can reach no other conclusion that what he observed was the result of paranormal activity.

As for never again experiencing any other unexplained phenomenon, I suspect that after witnessing the frightening incident with the phone, Randy may have deliberately avoided situations where ghostly activity may be able to sneak up on him, such as sitting alone in the dark, late at night, outside the Capitol Building's Old House Chamber.

Repeat Performance

What makes Lieutenant Randy Howard's experience with the phone more plausible, is the fact that the type of activity he experienced was not limited only to him. For, several years after Randy's paranormal incident, an almost identical disturbance was witnessed by Officer Brian Loving at the exact same location.

It was late one night during the fall of 2001, approximately one o'clock in the morning, and Brian, then a four-year veteran of the Virginia Capitol Police, was conducting one of his mandatory checks of the interior of the Capitol Building. Completing his long walk through the dark hallways and corridors of the building, Brian found himself in the second-floor Rotunda area, illuminated only by the small desk lamp, and sat down at the hostess desk where Randy Howard had years before witnessed his unnerving event.

Relishing the peacefulness of the Rotunda's midnight atmosphere, and unaware of Randy Howard's prior paranormal experience at the very place he now sat, Brian reached for the phone that lay in the center of the hostess desk and called home. Brian admitted during interview that this phone call took place during a turbulent period of his previous marriage, and it wasn't long before the conversation with his wife became quite heated. After carrying on a fiery exchange for several minutes, he abruptly ended the conversation and hung up the phone. At this point, with the tranquility of the Rotunda having been destroyed by his angry phone conversation, Brian turned to leave the area. But, as Brian stepped away from his chair, he was startled by the sight of the phone sliding slowly across the desk as if propelled by unseen hands. Astounded, he stood still and looked on as the phone continued to move slowly across the desk before falling off the edge and landing heavily on the marble floor.

Now shocked by what he had just witnessed, Brian struggled to rationalize what he had observed. There was absolutely no one in the Rotunda area with him, and there was categorically no reason why the phone could have moved across the desk on its own and fallen to the floor. Sensing that there was quite possibly some unseen force at work, Brian quickly replaced the phone on the desk and hurried down the stairs to the relative haven of the building's west entrance.

Later, while considering the event, Brian wondered why paranormal events would often occur around him. He never deliberately provoked any ghosts that may haunt the Capitol area, and he most certainly did not purposely seek them out. Brian did wonder if his heated phone conversation with his wife may have disturbed a restless spirit, causing it to make its presence known. Although, one element of the activity that wasn't such a mystery was the location in which it occurred. Bearing in mind the tragic history of the Old House Chamber, located directly behind the hostess desk, and appreciating how many people perished within its walls, it is not surprising that the area around the room generates such intense paranormal activity. For many who believe, it is not inconceivable that the tormented lost souls of the numerous victims of the disaster remain trapped within the location where their lives were so tragically and abruptly ended.

Disembodied Voice

When it comes to dealing with the paranormal, Sergeant Phil White is perhaps one of the most experienced officers within the ranks of the Virginia Capitol Police. If it is ever said that a person could be especially sensitive to paranormal activity, I believe Phil possesses the trait. For, amongst the ranks of the Virginia Capitol Police, Phil has by far experienced more unexplained phenomena than anyone else. And although hel has since retired from the department where he worked for almost thirty years, he can still recall many of his ghostly experiences as if they occurred only yesterday.

What also may have added to the frequency that Phil crossed paths with the paranormal is the fact that he worked more than twenty years of his service with the Virginia Capitol Police on the graveyard shift, beginning as a patrolman and retiring as a sergeant. And, of course, during his long tenure with the department, Phil spent numerous shifts alone within many of the Capitol's reputedly haunted buildings, providing ample opportunity to witness ghostly activity. It is no surprise, then, that Phil has so many interesting recollections of personal experiences with the other side, and a number of recollections of fellow officers' experiences, too.

One of Phil's notable experiences occurred around 1989 inside the Capitol Building. It was late at night and Phil had been standing at the west entrance when he was alerted to an audible alarm from the building's fire control panel, indicating a smoke detector had been activated in an area on the third floor. As it was policy for all alarms to be investigated, regardless of the amount of false alarms that tended to plague the building's fire control system, Phil grabbed his flashlight and hastily made his way towards the indicated area.

Reaching the top of the stairs that led to the particular area of the third floor, Phil immediately recognized an uncomfortable feeling of being closely observed and paused momentarily in order to adjust to the extraordinary atmosphere. Phil was by now no stranger to the building's unusual phenomena, and although not perturbed in the slightest by its apparent presence, was still cautious in his approach to the unknown. With senses on high alert, Phil continued to the area where he believed the activated smoke detector was located.

At this time of night, most of the lights within the building were off and only a few necessary lights remained on, so Phil used his flashlight to navigate most of his way around the third floor of the building. Checking the rooms on the north side of the floor, Phil then made his way to the area of the Governor's Office and Conference Room, where several rooms connected behind heavy, locked wooden doors. As he approached the doors that led to the locked offices, still aware of the feeling that his every move was being watched by some unseen presence, Phil suddenly heard the distinct whispering voice of a female asking, "Have you found it yet?" Stunned, Phil immediately looked around in an effort to see who was standing there with him, but there was no one there. Phil knew he had definitely and distinctly heard a woman's voice whisper the words to him, but there appeared to be no one else around. It had sounded like whoever was responsible for the voice had been right next to him when they spoke, but Phil was confident that there was no one else in the building.

Still bemused by the peculiar voice, Phil unlocked the door that led to the Governor's Office and made his way through the dark adjoining rooms, searching each room with his flashlight for anything that could have been responsible for the strange whisper. After discovering nothing that could explain the phenomena, Phil exited the room and relocked the door. Suddenly, he again heard the same distinctly female voice from just over his shoulder, only this time it clearly stated, "You won't find it; it's not here."

Phil, now quite startled by the apparent phenomena, again scanned the immediate area with his flashlight. There was no one else around, and although Phil was convinced that he was alone in the building, he definitely sensed the presence of someone, or something, close by, and he felt it was likely one of the building's ghostly inhabitants.

After double-checking the area for signs of anything that may have triggered the smoke-detector, Phil eventually made his way back down to the building's west entrance, confident that there was no genuine alarm, but also convinced that other, more unconventional powers were at play. Again, he had experienced the intense feeling that he had come to associate with the presence of paranormal activity, and again, he had experienced firsthand the mischievous behavior of an unseen entity. But, while others may have been troubled by the apparent strange phenomena that seemed to haunt the Capitol and other buildings in and around Capitol Square, Phil simply took the events in his stride and went about his duties, knowing that every now and then, the spirits that call Virginia's Capitol home like to make their existence known.

A Ghostly Gathering

Another strange event experienced by Phil White transpired a couple of years prior to the Capitol renovations. Phil was again working a graveyard shift at the Capitol Building and had been at his assigned post for a couple of hours when he began an interior check of the building. As Phil progressed throughout the first floor, scanning with his flashlight as he made his way towards the steps that lead to the upper levels, his senses were suddenly alerted to the sound of voices—many voices—chatting away in a room above.

Curious as to the origin of the voices, and with the knowledge that there was no one else in the building, Phil climbed the marble stone stairs to investigate. He reached the second floor and paused to listen in order to ascertain the location of the voices. Standing alone in the darkness, Phil could again hear the distinct sound, as if a group of men were conducting a meeting, apparently coming from the area of the Old House Chamber. So, flashlight in hand, Phil ventured towards the tall, heavy wooden doors that secured the room that has so often played host to reports of unexplained phenomena.

Reaching the locked doors, Phil continued to hear the sound of voices chatting away from within the darkened room, but again, heknew that it was unlikely that there was anyone inside. The voices were clearly audible, but sounded strangely muffled, as Phil unlocked the doors, and he was unable to hear exactly what was being said. But Phil had little doubt that the voices were coming from beyond the wooden doors of the Old House Chamber, and he was determined to find out one way or the other who was responsible for the chatter.

Entering the room, Phil was surprised to hear the mumbling suddenly cease. There was an icy chill in the air, and as Phil stood in the doorway, he sensed that something strange was at work. The statue of General Lee cast its long shadow across the room as the dim light that penetrated the doorway slightly illuminated the pitch-dark interior. Phil reached for the switches on the wall adjacent to the door and quickly turned on the lights. There was no one in the room. Phil knew that he had, moments ago, heard several voices, like a group of grown men conducting a conference, definitely coming from within the room. But there he stood, looking around the room, and there was absolutely no one around. Nor was there any sign of anyone having been there. There was only one entrance and exit to the Old House Chamber and Phil was standing in it. No one could have left the room unnoticed and there was nowhere for anyone to hide. So, comfortable in his own sanity and sure of what he heard, Phil turned off the lights, locked the doors, and continued his midnight tour of the rest of the building.

Phil completely trusted his instincts and after considering the familiar eerie sensation he had experienced upon entering the room, and the fact that the phantom voices had ceased the moment he had opened the Chamber's doors, he was content in the knowledge that he had again likely experienced paranormal activity. But once again, Phil remained unfazed by the presence of the paranormal and knew that, as a Capitol Police officer, dealing with the supernatural was simply part of the job.

Caught on Camera

Although most of the unexplained phenomena associated with the Capitol Building is reported to have occurred within the building itself, there have also been numerous reports of similar activity occurring within the surrounding grounds. One such event occurred right outside the Capitol Building and was witnessed by several officers who were monitoring a surveillance camera late one summer evening in 2008.

The incident occurred while Officer John Wilde, a twenty-one-year veteran of the Virginia Capitol Police, was training a new officer on the video surveillance system that utilizes several security cameras located throughout the Capitol complex. It was a dark, moonless night and John looked on as the new officer familiarized himself with the operation of the system. While focusing one of the cameras on an area of the exterior north-west portion of the Capitol Building, and the adjoining portion of the Capitol gardens, both officers' attention was suddenly drawn to a strange image on the monitor screen. The image appeared to be an intensely dark mass, about the size of a person, hovering several feet off the ground and moving at a reasonably fast pace away from the western portion of the Capitol. The image traveled several yards, across the road that circles the Capitol Building, and approached the landscaped lawn of the Capitol gardens. John asked the new officer if he, too, was witnessing what he was observing. Alerted by the level of excitement in John's voice, another officer, Joe, stared at the camera monitor, too, and now all three officers were looking intently at the strange dark silhouette on the monitor's screen.

As the three officers stared intently at the screen, they observed the dark spectral image, contrasted only by the few landscaping lights that surrounded the building, hover towards the bushes that line Capitol

Square's iron-railing perimeter fence, and vanish as quickly as it had appeared. Curious as to what they had all just observed, the officers questioned each other and it appeared that they had all witnessed the same image: an intensely dark mass approximately the size of a person, hovering several feet above the ground and moving briskly across the road and lawn.

At this point, John picked up the phone and called the officer who was on duty at the west entrance of the Capitol Building. He asked the officer if anyone, or anything, had just exited that end of the building or if he had noticed anything strange moving within the northwestern portion of Capitol Square. The officer at the west entrance had not seen anyone leave the Capitol Building, nor had he observed anything moving around the grounds. There was no breeze that night that could have propelled an object through the air, and a subsequent search of the portion of Capitol Square where the dark silhouette had disappeared also revealed nothing that could explain the ghostly image. So, short of a rational explanation for what he and the other two officers had just observed, John surrendered to the notion that what they had witnessed was quite possibly paranormal, as nothing else could explain the strange and intensely dark mass that had mysteriously floated through the grounds and disappeared.

The Orb

Another similarly strange incident that occurred close to the same location as the previous event was witnessed by Officer Brian Loving. It was late one Friday night, during the summer of 2000, and Brian had been working at the Governor's Mansion. At around one in the morning, Brian was relieved from his assigned duty post and walked over to the Capitol Building. Returning from the building several minutes later, Brian was walking down the stone sidewalk, approaching the north-facing portion of the exterior of the Capitol Building, when he had an extremely strange encounter.

As he walked around the corner of the building, Brian was astonished to notice a strange spherical transparent light, approximately the size of a small soccer ball, floating in the darkness about ten inches above the ground in front of him. Startled, Brian stood for several seconds in the dark shadow of the building and stared as the brightly lit object began to move slowly towards him. Brian recalls, at this point, being mesmerized by the yellowish-green light, but sensed no fear as the sphere of light began to move in tandem with him as he slowly continued the short walk back to the Governor's Mansion. As Brian approached the Mansion, still closely followed by the mysterious transparent orb of light, the light appeared to perform a wide fast-flying loop around him before seemingly abandoning its pursuit and quickly disappearing beyond the nearby trees.

Now completely freaked out by the mysterious orb, Brian hastily entered the gate of the Mansion grounds. The other two officers on duty at the location had witnessed the acrobatic display of the strange luminescent object and stood in disbelief at what they had observed.

One of the officers, Joe, asked Brian, "What the heck was that?" and the other officer, Chuck, added "Man, that was freaky!" as Brian ducked inside the perceived safety of the guard shack in an effort to regain his composure.

Glad that the light had abandoned its illuminating and mesmerizing display, Brian just stood and shook his head in amazement. He had no answer for either of them. He had absolutely no idea what the strange ball of light was, where it had come from, or why it had chosen to follow him to the Mansion gate. But, whatever it was, it was not normal, and all three men suspected that it was most definitely related to the strange and frequent paranormal activity that had become such a mainstay of the Capitol's historic precedence.

Never before had any of the officers witnessed such an astonishing display of apparent supernatural activity, nor have they since. However, as bizarre as the activity may seem, as paranormal energy appears to take many different forms, I consider it quite reasonable to conclude that what Brian, Joe, and Chuck witnessed on that dark summer night may possibly be a form of manifestation of whatever ghostly entity, or entities, allegedly haunt Virginia's historic Capitol Square.

Ghost of a Governor?

Having been the epicenter of Virginia politics since 1788, is it implausible that past politicians may return in the afterlife to visit the place where they once, with so much dedication, served the great Commonwealth? An event experienced by Officer Ken inside the

Capitol Building lends to the belief that the ghost of a former Governor may indeed haunt the area that may have once been his office and conference room.

The event occurred late one evening around 1998. Ken was performing the last checks of the interior of the Capitol Building and had made his way to the area of the Governor's conference room. The long narrow chamber lies adjacent to what was once the Governor's office and contains a long, hardwood antique conference table that sits prominently in the center of the room, surrounded by matching wooden chairs with leather upholstered seatbacks and cushions. Of course, everything inside the room matches the building's period architecture and design, including the framed portraits and brass light fittings that decorate the walls.

Late at night, the lights are generally off inside the room, and upon entering from the main door, the first thing a person usually notices in the glow of a flashlight is the polished table and the Governor's chair, the largest of all the chairs, sitting facing the door from the far end of the room. Due to the nature of the chair's leather upholstery, the wear of numerous Governors has formed a permanent imprint in the seatback that makes it look like an invisible person is sitting in the seat, especially when illuminated by only the glow of a flashlight. Most officers are familiar with this anomaly and are not in the least disturbed by it, but many have also wondered if there really *was* an invisible entity sitting in the chair, watching as they walked through the dark room and into the adjoining offices. On this particular evening, Ken was left wondering no more.

Ken opened the door to the interior of the Governor's conference room, shedding the outer floor's dim light on the pitch-dark room, and slowly scanned the darkness, searching for anything out of place. As his eyes peered to the back of the room, he was astonished to see an older white gentleman, with gray hair, wearing a dark suit with a white shirt, looking back at him from the Governor's chair. Momentarily startled by the unexpected sight, Ken reached around the door for the light switch, while at the same time flicking on his flashlight. But, as his flashlight illuminated the inside of the room, Ken was surprised to see that there was no one there.

Intrigued by what he had just observed, Ken entered the room and quickly checked the interior doors that access the adjoining offices.

Overlooking the Rotunda level, the doors
to the Governor's offices and conference
room are rumored to conceal some ghostly
occupants. *Photo by author*

As expected, the doors were all locked, and as Ken looked around the
room, he sensed an unusual chill in the air and he had an acute uneasy
feeling. So, securing the room and again turning off the lights, Ken
left the area and continued his checks.

Assessing in his mind what he had experienced, Ken was confident
that his eyes had not been playing tricks on him. He had definitely
seen an older gentleman sitting in the Governor's chair, facing the
door from the far end of the narrow room. Ken's only regret was that
he hadn't seen the apparition's face long enough to be able to compare
it to the many portraits of past Governors who adorned the interior
walls of the Capitol Building, possibly solving the mystery of which
former statesman's ghost appears to have revisited the Governor's
conference room.

The Renovations

It is widely believed throughout the paranormal investigative community that renovations occurring within a reportedly haunted location can instigate paranormal activity, either by triggering the manifestation of residual energy or by disturbing the restless souls that allegedly haunt a location. It is with little surprise, then, that there have been several reports of paranormal disturbances said to have occurred during the 2004 to 2007 renovation of Virginia's Capitol Building.

During the renovations, the interior of the Capitol Building was completely gutted. Walls, doors, and windows were removed, and floors were replaced, as construction crews with heavy equipment worked to restore the Capitol's interior as closely to its original layout as possible. Even the exterior of the building was replaced, as the crumbling centuries-old brickwork had begun to compromise the building's structural integrity. It is with little wonder that such a magnitude of change and work activity may have disturbed some of the spirits that wander the Capitol's halls.

Officer Jose DeJesus, of the Virginia Capitol Police, was one such witness to the apparent paranormal activity that occurred during the Capitol's renovation period. Jose recalls that on several occasions during the renovations, he would hear the sounds of people walking through the Capitol's lonely corridors during the dark midnight hours. He would hear the footsteps so clearly that he was convinced that they were being caused by living beings, and not, as it would appear, by the restless spirits of the dead. However, when he would respond to the area where the sounds seemed to be coming from, he would be unable to locate anyone or any signs of someone having been there; although, Jose does recall experiencing the strange feeling that witnesses often report sensing when in the close company of the paranormal.

On one occasion, during the graveyard shift, Jose was alone at the Capitol Building and was alerted to the sounds of voices seemingly coming from the central hallway. It was in the early hours of the morning and the only lights on within the building were small construction lamps that served to illuminate only certain areas, so, Jose flicked on his flashlight and proceeded to investigate the strange sounds. Only, as he made his way towards the center of the first floor, along the central hallway, Jose could see no one, but could hear the sounds of the voices moving further and further away. Like chasing a rainbow, Jose could never seem to reach the origin of the strange phenomena, although he could clearly hear the voices chatting away. Jose also noticed an unusual chill in the air and sensed he was not alone as the activity continued. But, as many times as he investigated the strange phenomena occurring during the renovations, Jose was never able to locate visible evidence of the presence of a ghostly entity. That is, until one cold winter's night when he investigated a suspicious situation beneath the stairs of the building's South Portico.

The event took place around two o'clock one morning when another officer had reported seeing a strange light emanating from the exterior area of a service door located beneath the South Portico steps. Even during the renovations, access was restricted to the interior of the building as much as possible and all exterior entrances and exits were secured, so light mysteriously appearing in an open doorway was considered cause for concern.

Jose and another officer responded to the location and began checking the immediate area surrounding the steps. It wasn't completely dark in front of the building, but the large and prominent marble staircase that climbed the front of the Capitol and overlooked the landscaped gardens cast dark shadows over the grounds below. As Jose and the other officer approached the east side of the portico steps where the service door was located, Jose couldn't help noticing a strange transparent mist hovering a couple of feet off the ground, slightly illuminated by a dim light emanating from the small open doorway. The gray mist appeared to be of no distinct form, but seemed a little thicker than fog, a few feet high, and a couple of feet wide. Its presence was completely isolated from the surrounding environment and appeared to be hovering stationary a few feet adjacent to the doorway. But although finding the phenomena strange, Jose assumed that the mist was simply a product of the environment and continued his investigation of the open door.

After reaching the door and finding no obvious cause for the strange light that was witnessed inside the doorway, Jose and the other officer re-secured the door and made their way back around the front of the portico steps. As they rounded the bottom wall of the steps, the officers were surprised to again notice the strange mist hovering in the darkness at the foot of the stairs. The mist appeared to be retaining its same blurry form and was still hovering above the ground, but it now appeared to be moving slowly westwards around the south portion of the building. Both officers watched with their flashlights as it continued slowly around the south face of the building and eventually disappeared.

What the officers considered most strange about the misty apparition was that it was moving against a slight breeze and had retained its form as it had slowly moved away from the area of the door and around the foot of the steps, a distance of approximately thirty to forty feet. After seeking a logical and rational explanation for the apparent phenomena, both officers concluded that there was nothing obvious in the area that could produce such a strange mist. Although skeptical, after some discussion, both officers agreed that it was plausible that the misty apparition was in fact paranormal in nature. As for the mystery light emanating from the doorway, it wouldn't be the first time ghostly lights have been reported around the Capitol.

The Dark Figure

Paranormal entities are often said to possess the ability to manipulate electronic equipment, such as causing fresh batteries in cameras to suddenly die and rendering high-tech detection devices useless. Some experts theorize that this is due to the entity drawing much-needed electrical energy from the surrounding environment in order to manifest itself, and could explain such commonly reported phenomena as temperature drops and chills. As this next encounter demonstrates, it seems that even the most modern surveillance systems can fall victim to supernatural influence.

It was summer 2010, and Officer John Fabian was on duty at the Capitol's west entrance. The time was approximately 11:48 p.m. and the graveyard shift officer who was due to relieve him was standing with John and another officer chatting about the day's events. The relief officer asked John if anyone was still in the building and John replied that the last two members of the cleaning crew had been the last to leave a while ago and that the building had been checked and there was no one left inside. John then referred the officer to the security system that clearly showed that the last two remaining cleaning staff had indeed swiped their electronic access cards upon leaving quite some time ago.

Looking puzzled by John's response, the third officer then pointed to one of the security camera monitors and stated to John, "I thought you said everyone was out of the building."

John and the other officer looked at the screen and were surprised to see the image of what appeared to be a tall person wearing a long black coat slowly walking away from the camera and down the corridor towards the Capitol's south facing Bank Street exit.

Suspecting that the person may have been an unauthorized intruder, John and the other officer quickly responded to the area in order to apprehend the individual. The third officer remained at the west entrance office to coordinate the search via the surveillance cameras while maintaining constant communication with John and the other officer over the police radio. The two officers rushed through the main corridor and down the narrow hallway and steps towards the Bank Street exit, but upon arrival were both a little astonished to see no one around. It was as if the suspicious person had simply disappeared.

Then, as if to add to their level of bewilderment, the third officer called over the radio that the figure he had been observing on the camera monitor had indeed disappeared.

"It's gone, just vanished," he said as he now viewed the two officers on the very camera monitor upon which he had only seconds ago been observing the strange person. Furthermore, the third officer also reported that none of the exit doors had been opened during the officers' response to the area and the camera covering the exterior of the Bank Street exit had shown no one leaving.

Growing concerned of the possibility of an unlawful intruder in the building, John and the other officer quickly formulated a search plan and began searching all of the rooms and offices in the immediate vicinity of the Bank Street exit. They knew that the person could not have left the area without being seen and it only stood to reason that anyone remaining in the area would have to be concealed within one of the adjoining rooms. After a thorough search, though, John and the other officer could not locate anyone. What John *did* notice was an eerie chill in the air and the sense that something was not as it seemed.

Having thoroughly exhausted all possible theories as to where the individual may have gone, the two officers returned to the west entrance to view the video footage. The third officer reassured the two officers that he had observed the image on the camera right up until he saw them both arrive in the area and then the figure had just simply vanished. It hadn't walked out of view of the camera, but instead had simply faded and disappeared before his eyes. In an effort to prove his irrational claim, the officer began rewinding the recorded footage on the monitor for John and the other officer to view. But, to their dismay, upon reviewing the footage, the officers were quite astonished to find that the digital recording only showed the period up until the strange image was first noticed and then skipped forty-five seconds to the point where John and the other officer arrived in the vicinity of the Bank Street exit. There was absolutely no saved camera footage of the strange person.

All three officers had clearly observed the individual on the camera monitor and all three were convinced that it was a tall person wearing a long, black coat. As far as they knew, the security system had never before stopped recording for no apparent reason, and no one else had reported any issues with the playback. So, why then had a person simply vanished before the officer's eyes and why did the camera-recording system act so strangely at the very moment a possible paranormal event occurred? Who knows? But, one thing is for sure, John and many of the other officers who have worked within the walls of Virginia's State Capitol are convinced that the strange activities are the work of something far beyond our realm of understanding and likely hold the answer to many of the building's suspicious activities.

Chapter 4

The Governor's Mansion

Better known as the Executive Mansion, the Governor's Mansion sits at the east end of Capitol Square, overlooked by the Capitol Building. The oldest occupied Governor's Mansion in the nation, the location has been home to numerous Virginia Governors and their families since 1813. During the Civil War, when Richmond was the Capitol of the Confederate States of America, the Mansion served as the center of state leadership and witnessed many historical moments and figures.

In 1863, after his death at the Battle of Chancellorsville, General Stonewall Jackson's body was laid in state at the Mansion until his funeral at the Capitol Building, and, in 1865, when Richmond fell to Federal troops, it narrowly escaped burning at the hands of fleeing Confederate troops. Since that time, the residence has continued to witness its fair share of historical moments, including visits by several U.S. Presidents and British royalty, and even a modern-day murder that occurred within its grounds.

Nowadays, the Mansion differs greatly from when it was first constructed and inhabited. Over the years, the building has undertaken many transformations at the hands of residing first families, and has experienced several face-lifts and renovations of both its interior and exterior. In 1999, during Governor Gilmore's administration, it underwent a multi-million-dollar renovation that saw the two front rooms restored as close as possible to their original 1813 appearance.

Although the Mansion is intended for Virginia's prestigious First Family, it is considered by many to be a lot smaller and less impressive in appearance than one might expect a governor's Mansion to be. The home consists of three floors, including a lower level, a historically

Shaded by centuries-old oak trees, the Executive Mansion sits prominently on the northeast corner of Capitol Square. *Photo by author*

restored and preserved first-floor area intended for entertainment of tourists, visitors, and guests, and a separate level for the First Family living quarters. Within the meticulously maintained grounds are several outbuildings that once served as servant quarters, kitchens, and stables, and now serve as staff quarters, offices, guest quarters, and a garage.

The Mansion and the several outbuildings on its grounds now exhibit a pale yellow painted exterior, similar to its earlier color scheme. Landscaped gardens, cobble stone sidewalks and driveways, and period architecture all help retain the location's traditional appearance. And, as a testament to its historical significance, the residence is also listed as a National Historic Landmark.

The Mansion Ghost

Although I have never read anything that substantiates the claim, it is rumored amongst the tour guides that sometime during the Civil War era, a young woman died in the Mansion after falling onto the cobblestone driveway from a horse-drawn carriage in front of the building. During my service with the Virginia Capitol Police, I heard this particular story from colleagues on several occasions—usually when they were recalling unexplained phenomena they claimed to have experienced within the Mansion grounds.

There are so many stories of paranormal disturbances originating from the Governor's Mansion that there have been several accounts published in local newspapers, magazines, and books, and many are well known to members of the Capitol Police. In fact, I'm sure there is not one Capitol Police officer who cannot recall some kind of ghost story originating from the location. One of the more popular stories told to me by a former member of the Capitol Police involves a previous Governor who had witnessed the ghostly apparition of a woman dressed in white in one of the upstairs bedrooms. Another even recalls how a Capitol Police officer came face-to-face with what may have been the same ghost, as he was descending the stairs within the residence. It is said that the officer was so traumatized by the event that he immediately quit his job. It is widely believed that the residence is indeed haunted by the ghost of a woman. However, during my own research on the paranormal activity, through conversations with my colleagues while I worked for the Capitol Police, and through my own personal experiences within the Mansion, I am quite surprised that the frequency and nature of the ghost's activity has not persuaded more witnesses to document their accounts.

When interviewing people in reference to their paranormal experiences, several mentioned having experienced strange events inside the Mansion. Some of the events described were convincingly paranormal in nature, but others were a little more questionable, even by the witnesses' own admissions. Although many of these smaller events could be quite easily explained rationally, some could also have been the work of ghostly entities.

Officer Jerry Chandler commented to me during an interview that he has on occasion, while working alone at night in the Governor's Mansion, experienced odd events that made him question his own skepticism. Jerry described how he had left the basement kitchen and returned moments later to find cupboard doors open or objects out of place that he hadn't noticed earlier while in the room. Of course, Jerry believes that it is quite possible that he simply may not have noticed the cupboards open, or objects out of place, prior to leaving the kitchen, but, the events did appear strange to him. Jerry even admits that, on other occasions, he has heard doors open and close while alone in the residence, and has heard phantom footsteps both within the Governor's Mansion and the rooms and corridors of the Capitol Building. However, Jerry still prefers to remain skeptical and says that he won't be convinced of the presence of ghosts around the Capitol until one materializes before his very eyes.

A Ghostly Welcome

My first strange experience within the Mansion occurred in July 2001, during my very first tour of its interior. I was training on the graveyard shift and had been led inside the building by a training officer, Kenny Perry. Kenny, a fifteen-year veteran with the Virginia Capitol Police, had shown me the first floor, with all its historically restored furniture and fittings, and had led me down the employee elevator to the basement level. As I stepped off the elevator, I noticed that the air felt strangely heavy, as if the surrounding air pressure had increased. I could sense the subtle pressure change in my ears, much like a person would experience when gaining altitude in an aircraft. It was a few seconds before the pressure equalized within my ears, leaving an audible whistling sound that lasted for several more seconds. There was no one else in the building, as the First Family was out of town, and the interior was deathly quiet except for Kenny's voice and our own footsteps. The lights were on in the basement area, but the narrow stone corridor that winds throughout the basement creates dark corners in the doorways leading to the offices and kitchen area. The corridor eventually leads past a tunnel entrance door and out into the central courtyard area of the grounds.

Kenny appeared not to notice anything unusual and kept up with the narrative of his guided tour as we continued down the corridor towards the exit and the outside courtyard. The air still felt heavy and the atmosphere a little strange as we passed by the stairs leading to the first floor when, all of a sudden, I felt an ice-cold draft on the back of my neck. The chill instantly traveled down my spine and the hairs on my arms and neck stood on end. I glanced up the extremely narrow staircase from where I had felt the cold chill originate from, but I did not notice anything unusual. All I knew was that I had the distinct and familiar feeling that we were not the only presences within the residence.

Kenny continued his narrative of the tour when he suddenly captured my attention with a statement about a ghost that allegedly haunts the Mansion. Now increasingly interested in what he had to say, I asked Kenny if he had ever experienced anything paranormal while working for the Capitol Police. His response was not surprising, and he briefly related to me several of his own and other officers' experiences with strange phenomenon within the residence—and other locations around the Capitol complex. He then cautioned me that I would routinely be left alone inside the Mansion and that I should learn to ignore many of the strange sights and sounds that can often be heard during the long nighttime hours; and not, like others before me, run terrified from the building.

At the conclusion of my tour, I informed Kenny of what I had experienced moments ago. He agreed that as we entered the basement area from the elevator he had sensed a strange atmosphere. He then informed me that it was not uncommon for new officers to experience something strange their first night on duty at the location. It was considered the ghost's way of welcoming newcomers to the residence.

From Kenny's brief recollection of his and some of the other officers' experiences, I concluded that most of the paranormal activity reported on the Mansion grounds was similar to that which allegedly occurred inside the Capitol Building. Claims of strange footsteps, disembodied voices, moving lights and shadows, and occasional full-bodied apparitions appeared to be quite common amongst the officers and Mansion staff who frequented the residence. I only hoped that the stories were the result of genuine paranormal activity and not the result of over-tired or over-active imaginations. I would soon find out for myself.

A Mysterious Light

Lieutenant John McKee has served as a Virginia Capitol Police officer since 1997. He was one of the officers who trained me when I first became a Police Officer in 2001 and has spent much of his time with the department as a member of the midnight shift. As a training officer, John was often tasked with mentoring new officers and familiarizing them with the state buildings and properties that fall under the jurisdiction of the Capitol Police.

It was in 1999, while showing a new officer, Steve Robinson, around the interior of the Governor's Mansion, that John experienced what he believes to be an encounter with the paranormal. As John recently told me the details of the incident, I could find no reason to doubt his account. Besides, how could anyone question his or any other witnesses' credibility when considering the sheer volume of other reported unexplained phenomena said to have occurred in and around the Governor's Mansion?

The incident occurred not long after the renovations to the Mansion were completed, during Governor Gilmore's administration. John was on duty at the location with another officer, Ken, and was tasked with taking the new officer, Steve, on a tour of the newly renovated interior of the residence. It was shortly after midnight and John and Steve left Ken at the guard shack at the front entrance to the grounds, unlocked the front doors, and began their tour. The Governor and his family were out of town on this particular night, and so, other than the two officers, there was no one else in the building.

Beginning their midnight tour of the premises on the first floor, John showed Steve the two front rooms that were restored to closely reflect their original 1813 appearance, and continued to the narrow staircase that led to the basement. Descending the basement stairs, John was keenly aware of the fact that they were all alone, as most of the interior lights were off and the rooms were deathly quiet.

Reaching the foot of the stairs, John paused to tell Steve some of the interesting historical facts concerning the residence, but as he began to speak, he was surprised to hear the distinct sound of heavy footsteps crossing the wooden floor directly above them. John simply assumed that another officer had entered the Mansion and was walking through the first floor, and so was not overly concerned by the sounds. But, as John heard the footsteps approaching the enclosed area of

The hardwood floors of the mansion's first floor are said to echo the footsteps of the building's paranormal residents. *Photo by author*

the top of the narrow staircase, he glanced up and noticed a strange bright stream of light cascade across the entrance at the top of the stairs. John, although intrigued by the seemingly strange nature of the light, assumed that the light was caused by either another officer's flashlight or the headlights of a car entering the Mansion grounds, and so continued the tour of the interior unperturbed.

After completing their tour, John and Steve exited the residence, re-locked the front doors, and joined Ken at the entrance to the grounds. John mentioned to Ken that he had heard another officer walking about the first floor and inquired as to who it was. Steve also commented to Ken that he too had heard the sound of footsteps on the wooden floor above their heads, but they were both surprised when Ken stated that no one else had entered the Mansion. He reminded John and Steve that John had taken the only set of keys to the building from the guard shack in order to gain access to the interior of the residence, so another officer could not possibly have accessed the interior. John was sure that they had locked the front door upon entering the residence, and they all knew that no one could have accessed the location without being seen, so all three officers were confused as to how both John and Steve had clearly heard the sound of heavy footsteps originating from the first floor. John was even more bemused by the fact that he had observed the beam of light that he had assumed was caused by an officer's flashlight passing by the entrance at the top of the basement staircase.

Intrigued by the mysterious events, John sought a rational explanation for the phenomena, but was unable to find one. The light he had witnessed at the top of the stairs was obviously not caused by another officer's flashlight, as another officer could not possibly have entered the Mansion. Upon further investigation, John also found it implausible that a car's headlights had been the cause of the strange light beneath the door. The door that enclosed the hallway at the top of the stairs had been closed at the time, and there was no exterior window on the first floor positioned in a way to allow the beam of a car's headlights to illuminate the top of the staircase. Therefore, lacking any credible rational explanation, John and Steve concluded that the events they had both experienced that night inside the location may have been another case of paranormal activity—activity that appears to be all too common in the Governor's Mansion.

Spectral Lights

Surprisingly, strange unexplained lights are not an uncommon occurrence within the Governor's Mansion. Several people have reported witnessing strange spherical lights moving around within the empty residence that, when investigated, could not be explained. Witnesses have reported observing the phantom lights both from within the Mansion and from outside, but opinions vary as to what the phantom lights may be. Some say they are ghostly candles being carried room to room by the phantom resident, and others say they are bright spectral orbs that are considered by some paranormal experts to be a concentrated form of spirit energy. Whatever the ghostly lights are, they seem to appear when least expected, and usually when no one else is home.

Officer Ken remembers witnessing the lights back in 1998, while on duty at the Mansion gate. Ken was the only officer on duty at the location, and was in fact the only person present on the property that night, as the First Family was out of town. He had checked the interior of the residence earlier in the night, and had turned off all the internal lights, leaving the exterior windows looking dark and lifeless.

It was in the early hours of the morning, around two-thirty, and Ken had stepped out of the guard shack for a breath of fresh air. Scanning the area for signs of anything unusual or out of place, Ken turned to face the front of the Mansion and was surprised to see a small light flickering against the darkness of one of the upstairs windows, casting a warming glow in the otherwise lifeless room. Looking intently at the window, wondering if the strange radiance was in fact a light from inside or simply a reflection from outside, Ken watched as the gleam appeared to move slowly from one window to the next, as if wandering from room to room. There are five west-facing windows on the second floor and Ken watched as the light, which he said appeared to flicker like a candle, slowly passed by each window as it crossed from one side of the residence to the other.

Concerned as to who, or what, may be causing the mysterious illumination, Ken summoned another officer to the guard shack before entering and thoroughly searching the interior of the building. Upon completing his search, Ken was unable to locate anything that could explain the mysterious light that he had minutes ago observed. There was no one inside the Mansion and there were certainly no candles lit, but there had been present the usual eerie sensation that most had become accustomed to while experiencing such anomalies—a sensation that had seemed to follow Ken through every room of the residence as he diligently searched for clues as to the origin of the ghostly glow. In the absence of any rational explanation, and fully aware of the residence's eerie reputation, Ken suspected that the spectral light was indeed quite possibly yet another unexplained phenomena related to the building's famed paranormal resident.

The Cold Room

Without a doubt, one of the most knowledgeable and experienced Capitol Police officers and witness to the Mansion's ghostly secrets has to be Mike Jones. Before retiring in 2007, Mike had served as the Assistant Chief of Police with the Capitol Police during my service with the department and had been an officer with the agency since the early 1980s. As a long-serving officer with the department, Mike has performed in almost every function of the Capitol Police while working his way up to the rank of major, and has walked every room and corridor within the Capitol complex many times over. So, it goes without saying that Mike possesses a level of experience and insight into the strange occurrences in and around Capitol Square that very few others possess.

While speaking to Mike in reference to this book, he commented that he was delighted that someone had finally documented the strange activity that has appeared to have plagued the Capitol area for as long as he can remember, activity that he himself has witnessed on several occasions. Mike further stated that as a former criminal investigator, and as such a rational thinking individual who relies on science to provide answers, he has always remained skeptical of the existence of the paranormal and would strive to exhaust every possible conventional explanation before ever considering a less-than-scientific theory. However, he admits that the longer he was with the Capitol Police, the more and more convinced he became of the possibility that modern science may not hold the answer to every seemingly strange occurrence and that it may be that there exists a realm beyond ours that defies the fundamentals of rational belief.

Mike also believes that in order to experience the paranormal, a person first needs to be open to the possibility of the existence of ghosts. He theorizes that if a person can "sense the deep history of a location," such as the Capitol and the Governor's Mansion, they may be far more sensitive to events and activity that may simply be ignored by others. Even he admits that during his many years with the Capitol Police, he has experienced few places that provide such an intense sense of history as that exhibited by the historical buildings located in and around Capitol Square. But, even as a believer in the paranormal, Mike prefers to remain skeptical of such claims and still relies on science to provide an explanation before resorting to the exploration of unconventional theories.

One of several paranormal events that Mike personally witnessed while serving with the Capitol Police occurred in 1983 while he was working the graveyard shift within the Capitol grounds. Mike had stopped at the Mansion in the middle of the night to check on the assigned officers and was talking to the officer at the gate when another officer, new to the Capitol Police, came rushing out of the front door of the residence. The First Family was out of town and the new officer had been alone in the basement kitchen area when he witnessed a brief glimpse of what he believed to be the ghost of a young woman dressed in white. Overcome with the sudden realization that there was no one but himself inside the building at the time, he quickly concluded that what he had seen was not of this world and subsequently panicked and ran for the front door.

Reaching the front gate and the company of Mike and the other officer, the new officer, visibly shaken, recalled the events that led to his hasty exit from the Mansion. Mike, of course, was skeptical and thought there might in fact have been someone else previously unknown to them staying in the residence, so he and the other officers conducted a thorough search of the premises.

Upon searching the dark interior of the building, the officers located no one. They searched every room but could not find any evidence of another person inside the home. But, what the officers *did* find out of the ordinary was the fact that the First Family's small dog was cowering and acting strangely nervous. Ever such a people-friendly animal, it was completely out of character for the dog to behave in such an unusual manner and it was duly noted by all those present.

What was also noticed by the officers was that the first-floor dining room felt at least twenty degrees cooler than the rest of the interior of the Mansion. In fact, it was so noticeably cold that Mike says he had a maintenance person check the heating and air-conditioning unit, but they reported that although the room felt excessively cold, they could find nothing wrong with the system. What also seemed odd about the whole experience was that the security system would have alerted the officers to the presence of anyone else in the residence should there have actually been a living person within. So, in the absence of a rational explanation, and considering the presence of the strange temperature anomaly and the dog's unusual behavior, Mike considered that there may be a presence in the Mansion that is not on any guest list—at least, not a guest list from recent times.

Murder at the Mansion

In January 1989, while working as an investigator, Mike was assigned the onerous task of investigating a murder that took place on the Mansion grounds. The unfortunate victim of the grisly act was a 61-year-old man who had worked at the residence as a groundskeeper since 1975. In all his years of faithful service to the Commonwealth, the man (known by his nickname Captain George) was a regular face around the Capitol Square area and was well known to all who worked there. Several of the officers, including Mike, became friendly with George and regularly engaged in conversation with him as he went about his duties.

George met his unfortunate and untimely demise at the hands of another groundskeeper while working in the Carriage House at the rear of the Mansion. He was brutally bludgeoned to death by his assailant and his lifeless body left for a fellow worker to discover. Of course, everyone who knew Captain George was shocked at the nature of the tragedy, but what they found equally shocking was the fact that a crime usually reserved for other areas of the vastly populated City of Richmond had occurred only feet away from where Virginia's First Family lived in the heart of the historic Capitol area.

Mike's unwavering efforts paid off and, after only a few short days, his investigation led to the arrest and subsequent conviction of Captain George's killer.

But although the short-lived mystery was swiftly solved and the murderer brought to justice, it may be that Captain George still felt that he had some unfinished business at the Mansion, or he had simply grown so attached to the location he worked within for so many years that he didn't ever want to leave. Either way, it appears that the officers at Capitol Police hadn't yet seen the last of Captain George.

A Message From Beyond the Grave?

It was 1995 and Mike was now serving as a Captain with the Capitol Police. It had been six years since the murder at the Mansion, but Mike had not forgotten the man known as Captain George, who was once such a frequent face around the Capitol grounds, or the circumstances of his demise. Still, Mike was a little surprised early one morning when a young officer who had been working the graveyard shift at the Mansion came to him with a strange message.

The young officer greeted Mike and informed him that an elderly gentleman had approached him at the location at around four o'clock that morning, introduced himself as Captain George, and asked the officer to tell Mike he said hello. A little taken back by the gravity of the message, Mike inquired as to the description of the elderly gentleman, and, much to his surprise, found that his features closely resembled those of the man he once knew as Captain George. Surely this could not have been the case, as Mike knew without any doubt that George had died back in 1989. After further investigation, Mike pondered the possibility that the message had come from beyond the grave and that Captain George had returned for a visit. To begin with, who would be walking around the Capitol area at 4a.m., which is coincidentally the same time of the morning George used to regularly arrive at work? And, why would anyone pretend to be Captain George and leave a message for Mike stating so?

Whatever the cause for George's apparent return from the other side, Mike believes that unfinished business may be a reason why some souls choose not to pass to the other side but remain in the world of the living, seeking some sort of conclusion in defiance of their untimely death. Who knows? But, in the absence of any rational answers to the mystery of Captain George's eerie reappearance and considering the paranormal history of the location, it's one theory in this case that Mike does not discount.

A White Night Dress

Another incident that causes Mike to believe there is more going on in and around the Capitol area than often meets the eye occurred at around three o'clock one cold winter's morning back in 1985. Mike was alone in the Mansion basement kitchen area while the First Family slept in their private quarters, and had been on duty there for a few hours. Mike had been catching up on the newspapers and magazines and was admittedly tired when his attention was suddenly drawn to what he believes was the bottom portion of a long white night-dress just disappearing out of view beyond the doorway that led from the kitchen to the interior hallway. Although the lighting throughout the interior of the Mansion was dim at that time of the morning, Mike says he believes he clearly saw the white dress as he glanced up from his reading material, his attention caught by the unusual sudden movement within the solitary confines of the kitchen. Not one to be easily unnerved, Mike quickly arose from his seat and attempted to follow what he assumed was a person wearing a night dress into the darkness of the corridor, but, to his dismay, there was no one there. Whatever, or whomever, it was had simply vanished into the gloom.

So convinced of what he just witnessed, Mike called-in the incident over his police radio and informed the other officers on duty that night that there may be something strange going on in the residence. A couple of other officers arrived in due haste and assisted Mike in conducting a thorough search of the entire premises. As usual, though, nothing out of the ordinary was located and it appeared the First Family had remained undisturbed throughout the peculiar incident.

Not one to jump to wild conclusions, Mike analyzed the incident over and over in his head, each time trying to come up with a rational explanation for what he had just experienced. Although he was admittedly tired, he believes in what he saw and is convinced it was not the result of tired eyes or an overactive imagination. Whatever it was, Mike wasn't the first, or the last, person to report similar events. He even says, "Every Governor who has resided in the Mansion has reported similar experiences." So, with so many reliable and credible witnesses reportedly observing the same apparition, how can such activity be ruled a figment of the imagination or tricks of light? In the absence of any solid rational explanation for such events, is it too much to consider the possibility of a less conventional answer?

Face in the Mirror

Officer John Wilde has been a Virginia Capitol Police officer for over twenty-one years, and has also had his share of encounters with the paranormal while working at the Governor's Mansion. During the period that Governor Wilder held office, 1990 to 1994, John had a couple of strange experiences within the residence that he said he will never forget—experiences that made him question whether there was in fact some truth to the many reports of paranormal activity that gave the location its ghostly reputation.

The first of John's experiences with the Mansion's supernatural resident occurred early one morning during the Wilder administration.

It was a little after five in the morning and John was tasked with collecting the morning newspaper from the delivery person and taking it to the Governor's living quarters, where he would place it on the kitchen table. This was an every-morning routine and John had performed this duty on many previous occasions without incident.

Being so early in the morning, it was still dark outside as John entered the Mansion through the large front doors. As he closed the doors behind him, careful to avoid making enough noise to wake the sleeping Governor, he made his way through the first floor to the stairs that led to the Governor's living quarters. Hanging on the wall, half-way up the stairs, is a large antique mirror that was probably one of the Mansion's original furnishings. It was in this mirror, on these same stairs, that a previously serving Capitol Police officer is rumored to have witnessed the apparition of a ghostly woman dressed in white, that frightened him so much that he quit his job.

Ascending the dimly lit stairs, morning newspaper in hand, John momentarily glanced up at the mirror and was startled by the clear image of a face of a young woman staring back at him. John immediately turned to look up the last flight of stairs, expecting to see a woman standing facing the mirror, but was again startled to discover there was no one there. John instantly looked back at the mirror, but now there was no one returning his gaze. It seemed that whoever he had moments ago observed in the old antique-looking glass had simply disappeared in the matter of a second.

A little disturbed by this event, and with the knowledge of the Mansion's ghostly reputation, John hurriedly continued to the Governor's kitchen and completed his task of delivering the newspaper before making a hasty exit from the residence. John realizes that it's possible for one's mind and eyes to occasionally deceive them, but he is also extremely convinced of what he witnessed. To this day, John swears that he absolutely observed the face of a young woman in that old antique mirror on the Mansion stairs.

Officer John Wilde, and the officer who was rumored to have quit his job immediately after witnessing the ghost, were not the only two people to have witnessed the apparition of the young lady in the antique mirror. Ken was alone in the basement checking the interior of the Mansion, late one night in 1999, when he heard the distinct sound of footsteps coming from the first floor above. It was during

The mirror above the stairs is said to have shown the reflection of a ghostly lady in a white dress. *Photo by author*

Governor Gilmore's administration, and the Governor and his family were out of town. Ken was sure that no one else was supposed to be in the building, and so he used his radio to alert his colleague at the front gate of the suspicious noises, before continuing to the first floor to investigate. Ken described the footsteps as sounding unlike the heavy footsteps of a male, but more like the lighter footsteps of a female walking briskly about the first floor.

Reaching the first floor, Ken was unable to get the lights to turn on. Locating the switch and flicking it on and off a few times, the lights simply would not turn on. Assuming a tripped breaker was responsible for the electrical issue, Ken turned on his flashlight and continued towards the stairs to the second floor. Half-way up the stairs, the beam of Ken's light illuminated the old antique mirror, and to his shock and amazement, Ken observed a young blonde haired lady reflected there, wearing a long white dress, and staring back at him from the glass.

Startled by the reflection, Ken instantly turned to look up the stairs, expecting to see the person whose image was so clearly showing in the mirror, but in the darkness of the second floor, there was no one there. Looking back at the mirror, the image was gone, and Ken felt a cold chill run down his spine as he quickly realized what he had observed.

It was well known that the Mansion was allegedly haunted by a ghostly lady in white, and Ken was now convinced of it by what he had just witnessed. He felt there was no mistake as to what he had seen, as he knew there was no one else in the residence, and he also knew that people don't just disappear. Upon a later inspection of the Mansion's electrical room, no reason could be found for the power failure that Ken reported to have occurred moments prior to the ghost's materialization in the old antique mirror above the stairs.

A Ghostly Visitor

Another strange event witnessed by Officer John Wilde, within the halls of the Governor's Mansion, also occurred during the Governor Wilder administration. It was a little after four in the morning and John was on duty in the basement of the Mansion, sitting in what was once an old laundry room, but had later been converted into a butler's office. Being the only person in that area of the residence, John was a little surprised to hear what sounded like a woman's footsteps approaching the butler's office from the hallway beyond the office door.

John described the footsteps as sounding like those of women's shoes with high heels, as the metal tips of the heels were making a familiar sound on the stone floor of the hallway. Expecting to be visited by whomever it was that was coming towards the office, John rose from his chair and hollered, "hello," but there was no response. Now hearing the footsteps close to the door of the office, John again called out, "hello," but to his surprise there was again no response and the footsteps just simply ceased right outside the office door.

At this point, John walked curiously towards the office doorway to see who was outside, but as he stepped towards the door, he heard the footsteps hurriedly make their way back down the hallway, away from the butler's office. John immediately stepped out into the narrow corridor and followed the footsteps, but he was shocked that he could not see anyone who could possibly have been responsible for the sounds. Standing alone in the hallway, John was suddenly aware of an icy chill in the air and the hairs on the back of his neck stood on end. He had definitely heard the footsteps, but there was absolutely no one else in that area of the Mansion, and at this point, unable to locate anyone else in the residence, John considered the possibility that he may have had another experience with the resident phantom—a phantom that appeared to like catching the attention of the police officers that watched over the location during the lonely nighttime hours.

What makes this event more intriguing is the fact that John is not the only witness to the phantom footsteps who has recalled them as sounding like those of a woman's high-heeled shoes. Sergeant Phil White also has encountered the footsteps while alone late at night in the basement area of the Mansion. Phil stated that he was in the old kitchen in the basement and definitely heard what sounded like the clicking of a woman's high-heeled shoes approaching his location from the far end of the basement's stone corridor. So convinced was he that someone was walking down the corridor that he rose from his chair, assuming that the mystery lady was searching for him. But, after stepping into the corridor, he was amazed to discover that there was no one there. Only an icy chill remained in the air and the strange feeling he was not alone.

The Lady in White

It seems that there have been several witnesses to the reported ghost of a young lady in a white dress that allegedly haunts the Governor's Mansion. From police officers and visitors to the residence, to the young grandson of a previously serving governor, there is a host of convincing testimony that leads to the assumption that the ghost is indeed that of a young lady in a white dress. But, by far the most convincing testimony comes from Phil White, who not only heard the ghostly footsteps, but witnessed the mysterious entity in its entirety.

The event occurred sometime during Governor Allen's term of office (1994 to 1998), as Phil was working a graveyard shift assigned to the Mansion. Phil had been inside the building for a couple of hours and it was now the early hours of the morning when he decided to perform a cursory check of the residence's interior. The First Family was out of town and the Mansion was deserted as Phil began his check. Most of the lights were off and only a few necessary lamps remained lit, casting a faint glow throughout the serene interior.

Phil had begun his checks on the first floor and was making his way through the central hallway when he glanced up the stairway to his left and was startled to notice the figure of a young slender-looking lady dressed in a long white dress walking slowly up the stairs to the second floor. Phil instantly stopped, surprised by what he was witnessing, and attempted to rationalize what he was seeing. Maybe he was wrong in his assumption that the residence was indeed deserted and the young lady was simply a member of the Governor's family. But, in the back of his mind, Phil also sensed that what he was observing was not normal and he was again overcome by the familiar sensation that something strangely paranormal was at hand.

The young woman continued slowly up the stairs, apparently unaware of Phil's presence, and at this point Phil decided that the best course of action was to follow her in an attempt to ascertain exactly who she was and what she was doing there. Phil slowly, and a little reluctantly, began climbing the stairs, and as he reached the landing, situated halfway up the staircase, he glanced towards the top of the stairs and there stood, staring at him as he paused, the young woman in the white dress. Phil described her as being in her twenties, quite pretty, and dressed in a brilliantly white dress that appeared whiter than he had ever seen white before. She just stood there smiling at him from the top of the stairs. Phil recalls that it felt like a long time, but it was in reality probably only a few seconds before she broke her gaze, turned, and walked off into the darkness of the second floor. For a moment, Phil just stood there on the landing, mesmerized by the realization of what he had just seen, but after regaining his composure, he continued to the second floor.

Standing on the second floor, staring into the darkness, Phil could not see anyone. The image had seemingly disappeared. He still felt aware of a presence other than his own, so just to make sure, he conducted a thorough check of the entire living quarters. He found no one. Phil was again alone in the residence, not sure as to why the entity had chosen to appear before him, but convinced that whatever the reason, the experience had taught him that there are things going on inside the Mansion that are far beyond rational explanation—things that, in order to fully understand, require a person to possess a certain level of appreciation for the unearthly coupled with a unique ability to control their fears. For, as Phil has learned from numerous encounters with the unknown, there is little to fear of the paranormal but fear itself.

This wasn't the only time that Phil encountered the apparition of the young woman. Several years before witnessing her presence on the stairs, Phil observed what he believes may have been the *Lady in White* standing in an upstairs window of the residence late one night when the Mansion was empty.

Phil had been assigned to the Mansion gate, located at the front entrance to the grounds, and had already checked the interior of the residence and ensured that there was no one inside. The First Family was again out of town and therefore all the interior lights were off, leaving the residence in a relative state of tranquil darkness. All of the exterior doors were locked and Phil had settled in to what he expected to be another uneventful night at the Executive Mansion. The only illumination within the surrounding grounds was the dozen or so landscaping lamps that surrounded the residence, creating a ghostly glow around the base of the building. The front windows of the building were dark and so Phil's attention was easily captured as a light appeared to flick on and off in a bedroom located in the upper front portion of the residence. The exact window where Phil noticed the light was the center window above the front door, a room known as the Jefferson bedroom, and Phil recalled seeing the light come on for at least a second or two before going off again.

With the knowledge that there was no one inside the residence, Phil assumed that there may be some sort of electrical issue and decided to check on the area in case there was a more critical problem. But, upon inspection of the Jefferson bedroom, Phil was unable to locate anything that could explain the mysterious light. Content that there were no electrical issues occurring within the Mansion, but while also realizing the likelihood he was not quite alone, Phil re-secured the residence and returned to his post at the gate.

About an hour later, around two or three in the morning, Phil was again at the Mansion gate and turned to glance at the front of the residence. As he looked up towards the second floor, he was shocked to see a person standing in the window of the Jefferson bedroom. Phil was sure that there was no one inside the residence and stared at the figure as it just stood there motionless, looking out into the night sky. Phil described the figure as being white in color and the same size and shape as a person, but due to the low amount of light he could not clearly see any descriptive details such as clothing or facial features. The figure stood in the window for what seemed like a couple of minutes before gradually fading away and disappearing as Phil looked on.

Phil, of course, initially assumed that the apparition was simply a reflection in the window and looked around for a possible source. Not finding any and unable to draw any rational explanation for the image, he concluded that the figure could quite possibly have been the same entity that was responsible for the earlier manipulation of the bedroom light. But, whatever it may have been, after another thorough check of the interior, Phil was confident no one else was responsible as the Mansion was indeed completely deserted of all living residents.

The Phantom Butler

Although most of the ghostly goings-on around the Executive Mansion have been reported to occur within the residence, it is not unheard of for strange activities to be witnessed outside of the Mansion, within the walled confines of its grounds.

At the main entrance to the Governor's Mansion grounds is located a guard shack, where officers of the Virginia Capitol Police are stationed in order to welcome guests and visitors to the grounds and coordinate security screening of all those who request admission. The shack is small, but large enough to accommodate two police officers at any one time, and has large windows on all four sides that provide a panoramic view of the Mansion, the grounds, and the north and east portions of Capitol Square.

The guard shack is occupied 24/7 and has been the location of several reported paranormal events, ranging from moving shadows and objects, to full-blown apparitions. Sergeant Phil White recently recalled to me how on one dark night, while standing alone outside the guard shack, he witnessed a ghostly apparition standing close by him.

Phil had stepped out to smoke a cigarette and, in the darkness, noticed something standing off to his right side, beneath a tall oak tree that once stood overlooking the Mansion Gate. When he turned to see what it was, Phil found himself staring at the apparition of a tall, heavy-set, older African-American gentleman with a thick gray beard, and dressed in a black suit with a white shirt. He described the figure's dress as resembling that of a butler, and felt that this apparition may very well have been the Mansion's butler at one time. The figure didn't move, but only stood there beneath the tree, staring straight ahead into the darkness, as if waiting for something to happen. So clear was the apparition that Phil didn't even realize the figure was in fact a ghost until it disappeared before his eyes, causing Phil to drop his cigarette and retreat back inside the guard shack.

Although he states that upon first noticing the apparition he never realized it was a ghost, Phil did mention that it only took a split second before he recognized the strange but familiar feeling that tends to accompany paranormal activity, and was therefore instantly convinced that the person he was staring at was not of the living.

It would appear that the Governor's Mansion may be haunted by more than one ghost: a ghost of a young woman and the ghost of the butler. Many have reported witnessing the apparition of the young woman, or the distinct sound of her footsteps wandering the Mansion's halls, but only a couple of people have reported seeing the butler's ghost—Sergeant Phil White, and later, Sergeant Kenny Perry. However, that doesn't mean the ghost of the butler is less active, as it could be that some of the activity attributed to the phantom woman could in fact have been the activity of the mysterious butler.

Kenny reported witnessing the butler's ghost one summer's night back in 1996 while checking the Mansion's interior. The building had been locked up for the evening, as Governor Allen and his family were out of town, and Kenny was tasked with performing one last check before being relieved by the oncoming midnight shift.

Entering the Mansion through the basement kitchen door, Kenny made his way to the kitchen where he would begin his checks. As he rounded the corner to the kitchen, he heard a strange sound, like a person moving around, down at the end of the corridor that leads to the Mansion's exterior courtyard. Assuming that the exterior door had probably been left open, letting in the breeze, Kenny turned on the lights and made his way down the narrow stone hallway to the exterior door. As Kenny reached the door, he checked and found that it was secure, and so turned to walk back towards the kitchen. As he turned, he noticed a tall, black, older-looking gentleman, dressed as a butler in a black and white tuxedo-style suit, complete with white gloves and shirt tail. The gentleman walked slowly from one of the offices at the end of the corridor, towards the kitchen, and disappeared from Kenny's view as it turned the corner.

Kenny knew that there was not supposed to be anyone in the Mansion, and he also didn't recognize the butler as the one who currently worked there, but he didn't dismiss the fact that it was possible that another employee might have been working late. So, Kenny walked briskly back up the narrow corridor and attempted to catch up with the mysterious person.

Reaching the area where he had just observed the butler, Kenny could not locate anyone. He quickly searched the basement area, but still could not find anyone. He called the other officer, who was at the Mansion Gate, and asked him if anyone had entered the residence, but the other officer assured Kenny that he had not observed anyone coming to, or leaving from, the property.

Eventually, Kenny had searched the entire Mansion from top to bottom, but could not understand how a person could simply have disappeared. He had heard the stories of the resident ghost, but was under the impression that the ghost was that of a young woman, not an old man in a butler's suit. Puzzled, but intrigued, Kenny kept the strange experience to himself. It was only later that he heard from others at Capitol Police that Sergeant Phil White had also observed what he believed to be the ghost of the previous Mansion butler, adding a new twist to the mystery and suggesting that there was more than one restless spirit roaming the residence and grounds of the Governor's Mansion.

A Mischievous Entity

Another event that leads to the belief that paranormal activity at the Executive Mansion is not confined to the interior of the residence is one that occurred in the fall of 2007, to Officer Brian Alexander.

At around nine-thirty, one cold, dark evening, Brian was on duty at the Mansion Gate, and had been alone at the Gate for several minutes after relieving another officer for a coffee-break. Inside the guard shack, the interior lights were off, so as not to create a reflection on the interior of the glass, and Brian was sitting in the office chair intently watching the camera monitors. The white office-style desk that supports the camera monitors and computers inside the guard shack has several drawers and is situated in front of the officer's chair. Brian was sitting back away from the desk in the gloom of the guard shack when, all of a sudden, his attention was grabbed by the sight of the middle drawer of the desk suddenly and forcefully opening as if being pulled by unseen hands. The drawer jerked as it reached the limits of its rails and Brian instantly sprang up from his seat. A little shocked, but more bewildered by what he had just witnessed, he stared for a few seconds at the open drawer. He knew he hadn't accidentally touched or knocked the drawer, possibly causing it to open, but he also knew what he had just seen.

Hoping to find a rational explanation, Brian attempted to recreate the event. He closed the drawer to see if it would open again if knocked slightly or assisted in any way, but he was unable to get the drawer to open as easily or as forcefully as he had just witnessed. Brian was absolutely convinced of what he had just seen, and he was also convinced that the speed and action of the drawer opening was consistent with being forcefully pulled open by human hands, but none were seen and there was no one else in the guard shack at the time.

After several attempts at recreating the mysterious opening of the drawer, Brian surrendered to the notion that there was quite possibly no rational explanation for what he had just witnessed. And, as a ten-year veteran of the Virginia Capitol Police, Brian concluded that the incident could be paranormal, as it seemed to reflect the seemingly mischievous nature of activity that he had heard about from numerous other witnesses.

Another example of the ghost's apparent mischievous nature was witnessed by myself and Officer Jerry Chandler, shortly after we both began working for the Virginia Capitol Police. It was just after midnight one night, around July or August 2001, and we had both been tasked with checking and securing the interior of the Governor's Mansion. The First Family was out of town and another officer, Dave, remained at the Mansion Gate guard shack while Jerry and I went inside.

Entering the residence through the front door, Jerry locked the door behind us before we began our tour of the interior. We checked the first floor, stopping to view some of the historical artifacts and furnishings that adorn the two restored front rooms, and eventually made our way back to the main entrance after circling the entire first floor. Arriving back in the front lobby, we were both a little surprised to notice that one of the heavy wooden doors was slightly ajar. Jerry asked me if I had heard anyone entering the residence and I responded that I had heard no one. Both assuming that we had accidentally left the door unlocked, we closed the door, ensured it was properly locked, and resumed our check of the interior.

After completing a thorough check of the interior of the residence and finding no one inside, we both exited the Mansion through the basement and made our way back to the guard shack at the front gate. As we arrived back at the front gate, Dave asked us if we were going to close and lock the front entrance. We both knew that we had locked the front doors prior to resuming our check of the Mansion, so, puzzled by his request, we both turned to look. To our amazement, one of the two front doors was again open—not wide open, but open a couple of inches and letting out enough light through the gap to illuminate a portion of the stone doorstep.

Intrigued, Jerry and I returned to the entrance to investigate, but after closing and locking the entrance several times and pulling on them from both inside and outside, we were both unable to get the doors to open, nor could we find any evidence of a broken lock or latching mechanism. Returning to Dave at the front gate, we asked him how long the door had been ajar. Dave stated that he had seen the door open up only a couple of minutes prior to our return to the front gate. But, Jerry and I both knew that we had been in the basement for several minutes prior to exiting the Mansion, and there was no one else in the residence. We also knew that we had both exited the Mansion through the basement, so we were a little confused as to who could have opened the front door.

Several of the rooms on the first floor of
the Governor's Mansion have been restored
to reflect their original 1813 appearance.
Photo by author

Lacking any rational explanation for the mysterious opening and unlocking of the Mansion's front doors, not once, but twice, Jerry and I entertained ourselves with the notion that it could have been the famed Mansion Ghost that had mischievously unlocked and opened the door. Though we were new to the ranks of the Virginia Capitol Police, we both surmised that it would probably not be the last time we would encounter the mysterious activity that allegedly plagues the Governor's Mansion and its grounds.

The Window

Apparently, the Mansion Ghost's mischievous nature is not only limited to the movement of drawers and doors, but windows, too. Steve Robinson, now a Lieutenant with the Virginia Capitol Police, recently informed me of an incident he experienced a few years ago while checking the interior of the residence.

The incident occurred late one night during the graveyard shift as Steve was locking up the Mansion in the absence of the First Family. It was around twelve-thirty in the morning and Steve had made his way to the second floor, checking all interior rooms and offices and ensuring that none of the exterior doors and windows were left unlocked. Entering the kitchen, Steve noticed that the small wooden-framed window was partially open and promptly closed it and ensured it was locked. After establishing the residence was secure, Steve exited the Mansion and began checking the exterior grounds.

As Steve made his way around the Mansion's landscaped gardens and grounds, he glanced up and was surprised to notice that the kitchen window that he had moments ago secured was somehow open again. Curious as to how the window had apparently opened by itself, Steve reentered the dark and deserted residence and made his way up the staircase to the second floor. Upon reaching the second floor, Steve remembers feeling a little uneasy in the residence and the hairs on the back of his neck stood on end. He slowly made his way to the kitchen and found that the small window was indeed open, but, not one to become rattled by such apparent unexplained activity, Steve again closed and locked the window and performed another cursory check of the Mansion's interior. Finding nothing else strange and absolutely no one else inside, Steve once more secured the residence and returned to the Mansion Gate.

While recounting this experience, Steve mentioned that although he has over the years worked numerous graveyard shifts within many of the Capitol's reputedly haunted buildings, he has experienced no further unexplained phenomena. He further stated that what stands out in his mind about this incident is the way he remembers feeling inside the Mansion when returning to lock the window. He mentioned that although he hasn't had the feeling since, he definitely remembers an unforgettable and uncomfortable awareness of a strange presence within the darkened interior of the residence, and while he did not personally witness anything he considers conclusive evidence of the existence of ghosts around the Capitol complex, Steve does not dispute the fact that many of the Capitol's historic buildings may indeed be host to some kind of strange energy—the kind of strange energy that gives people the chills and makes objects go bump in the night.

Things That Go *BANG!* In the Night

By late 2002, I had been working for the Capitol Police for more than a year, and was by now quite unfazed by the unexplained phenomena that frequently occurred in and around Capitol Square. One night, though, during the graveyard shift, I had an experience inside the Governor's Mansion that gave me such a sudden fright that I spilled my coffee. I laugh at the recollection now, but at the time I didn't find the incident at all amusing.

I remember the incident quite clearly. It was a cold, wet wintry night, and after patrolling the grounds of the Mansion, I went inside to get a hot cup of fresh coffee from the basement kitchen. There was no one in the residence that evening, as the First Family was again out of town. The Mansion was locked up and only the most necessary interior lights had been left on. I unlocked the door to the basement and entered the residence, welcoming the sudden waft of warm air and absorbing the aroma of fresh coffee coming from the kitchen. Coffee was a necessity on the graveyard shift, and the Mansion's coffee was regarded as some of the best.

Entering the kitchen, the deathly silence from within the Mansion was interrupted only by the humming of the refrigerator and the occasional chirping of my police radio. As I stood in front of the coffee maker, my senses suddenly became increasingly aware of the ever so familiar feeling that I was not alone. I looked around as I stood pouring my coffee, but could not see or hear anything that would indicate that there was someone else in the residence. However, just to make sure, I picked up the phone attached to the wall above the coffeepot and called my co-worker, who was outside manning the guard shack at the entrance to the Mansion grounds. My co-worker answered the phone and I asked him if anyone had entered the residence since I had come inside. He assured me that the Mansion was indeed empty and then asked if I could bring him a coffee, too.

Satisfied that no one else had entered the Mansion, I hung up the phone and continued to pour the coffee. All of a sudden, there was a loud, thunderous *bang!* from an area of the basement around the corner from the kitchen. The loud bang sounded like a heavy, wooden door being slammed shut with considerable force, and was so audible that I felt the vibration in the floor, causing me to jump with fright and spill coffee down the front of my dark-blue uniform jacket and all over the floor.

Momentarily stunned, I was now staring in the direction of the loud bang with my flashlight in one hand and my other hand on my gun. I knew there was no one else inside the Mansion, and in a conscious effort to dismiss the possibility of paranormal activity, I tried to convince myself that the sound was more likely caused by either the wind or a living person—and it was my duty to establish which—so, staring into the darkened corridor and towards the glass doors of an interior office, aware of no other sound but my own heartbeat, I slowly made my way towards the area where I believed the noise had originated.

The narrow corridor became brightly lit by my flashlight as I continued towards the source of the loud noise. To my left, the corridor made a ninety-degree turn and I assumed that whoever, or whatever, had caused the loud bang was likely around this corner. I nervously peered around the edge of the wall, but as I had expected, there was no one there. The corridor was dimly lit, but I could easily see that there was nothing out of place, and there were no wet footprints on the brick floor that would indicate someone had entered the corridor from the outside courtyard area where it was raining hard. It felt cold in the corridor, but it tended to always feel a little cool in that area of the basement due to the brick floor and stone walls, a throwback to the Mansion's original construction.

I nervously checked the doors that led off of the corridor and verified that they were secure. I even entered a couple of the offices and ensured that there was no one hiding. My main concern was for the possibility of an unlawful intruder, and in my mind, I prioritized that it was my duty to ensure the integrity of the security of the residence. In the back of my mind, though, I sensed that I could possibly have just experienced the activity of the famed Mansion Ghost. I only hoped that now that it had obviously made its presence known, it would discontinue its activity for the remainder of the night, or at least until I had calmed my nerves and mopped up the spilt coffee.

I found nothing out of place in the Mansion and no rational explanation for the noise. With two fresh cups of hot coffee in my hands, I once again secured the basement door and joined my colleague in the guard shack at the entrance to the grounds. I didn't tell him what I had just experienced, because I knew that at some point during the cold, wet, and dark early morning hours, it would be his turn to enter the residence and fetch the coffee.

Haunting Activity

Tutti, as he is known to just about everyone who works in or around the Governor's Mansion, has worked as the Mansion's butler for more than twenty-five years. During that time, he has been witness to more than his fair share of paranormal experiences and has become quite used to the frequent unexplained phenomena, and the accompanying ghost stories, that appear to have become such a focal point of the Mansion's historic attraction.

As a long-serving member of the Mansion's staff, Tutti has also witnessed the comings and goings of numerous Virginia Governors and First Families, and has been privy to the personal experiences of the people who have at one time called the Mansion home. Without delving into the private lives of those he has served, Tutti did relate to me the details of several paranormal experiences allegedly witnessed by previously serving Governors and their families.

One such event was experienced by a previously residing Governor and his four-year-old grandson. The Governor had stated to Tutti that he saw his grandson apparently talking to an unseen entity on the Mansion stairs. When the Governor asked his grandson who he was talking to, the young boy simply replied that he had been talking to the lady who was standing at the top of the flight of stairs leading to the second floor. The Governor had, of course, seen no one on the stairs, as his grandson carried on his seemingly one-person conversation. After questioning the boy, the child remained adamant that he had been talking to a young lady who had been standing at the top of stairs. He even described her as wearing a long, white dress that had what he described as strings around the neck, considered to be the young boy's articulation of a lace neck-piece that was typical of Civil War-period dress.

Although those who had knowledge of this unusual incident, including the Governor, found the event strange, they did not dismiss the fact that maybe children have a unique ability to see and communicate with ghostly entities that cannot be seen or heard by adults, a theory that is commonly shared by many experts in the paranormal field.

Another phenomena said by Tutti to have been experienced by a previously residing Governor involved the mysterious lighting of a light bulb that hung at the top of the stairs on the second floor. According to the Governor, the bulb would mysteriously come on at the same time every night without anyone touching the switch, and, as far as Tutti knows, the mystery of the self-illuminating light bulb was never solved.

However, what is quite possibly the strangest paranormal behavior alleged to have been displayed by the Mansion's most famous resident was witnessed by Tutti and several other long-serving members of the Mansion staff. The activity has allegedly occurred quite frequently throughout Tutti's years of service at the Governor's Mansion. According to Tutti, he had heard from several other employees at the residence that they often witnessed a television in one of the old guest bedrooms turn on by itself, and, as if the nature of the activity in itself was not strange enough, the television would turn on at the same time every day, twelve-thirty in the afternoon, always on Channel 6, and coincidently during the daily airing of TV's *The Young and the Restless*.

Tutti, being a rationally minded person, was initially skeptical of the reports of the activity surrounding the television, and probably assumed that it was one of the staff, and not the ghost, that was a fan of daytime TV. But, as Tutti recalled during a recent conversation, sometime between 1986 and 1990, during Governor Baliles' administration, he witnessed the phenomena for himself while alone in the guest room containing the TV. Seeing no ghostly apparition to support the phenomena, though, Tutti just simply dismissed the activity as an electrical issue and went about his work unperturbed. Of course, back then, TVs in the Mansion were not capable of being programmed to automatically come on at a certain time, and the buttons and switches on the old TVs required a deliberate amount of pressure to manipulate them, ruling out many possible rational explanations for the phenomena. Although none of the staff ever reported physically seeing a ghostly apparition turn on the TV, it is with a degree of certainty that the staff concluded that the phenomena was the result of the Mansion ghost's mischievous nature, always seemingly trying to get the attention of those who work inside the residence, while coincidentally appearing to be a fan of daytime TV shows.

A Spooky Distraction

Another person who is no stranger to the ghostly goings-on in the Governor's Mansion is Maria Logan, an employee at the residence since the early 1990s. Maria recently talked to me about her numerous experiences with the Mansion's resident specter, and also surprised me with an account of an incident that happened only recently—coincidentally, the day before Halloween 2009.

It was the middle of the day, and Maria was intending to make her way to the second floor of the residence. As usual, Maria summoned the elevator to the basement in order to take her and her cleaning equipment to the second floor. But, stepping onto the elevator, she was dismayed to find that the elevator would not go up. Assuming that it was out of order, Maria climbed the stairs to the second floor.

Upon reaching the top of the stairs with her equipment, Maria was surprised to hear the familiar bell-chime indicating that the elevator was arriving at the second floor. Only a couple of minutes earlier, she had been unable to get the elevator to work, but now it appeared to be working fine. Moments after the empty elevator's arrival at the second floor, Maria observed its doors close once more and descend to the lower floors. Seconds later, as suddenly as it had descended, the elevator returned to the second floor. Bemused, Maria watched intently as it again closed its doors, without anyone having been on it, and made its way back down to the lower levels. At this point, suspecting a mechanical issue with the elevator, Maria contacted one of the maintenance staff and informed them of its apparent malfunction.

After inspecting the elevator, a technician could find nothing wrong with it. Maria assured the technician that the elevator had been acting strangely, but the technician was confident that there was no mechanical malfunction and Maria returned to her work on the second floor, hoping that the problem had resolved itself.

Upon returning to the second floor, Maria was again surprised to see the elevator arrive, again with no one on it, and immediately close its doors and descend to the lower floors. Maria then recalled previous similar experiences with the elevator and also remembered that its curious behavior was usually accompanied by other unexplained phenomena, presumably the activity of the Mansion ghost. Of course, Maria also realized the relevance of that day's date, October 30th, one day before Halloween. So, without further ado, Maria collected up her equipment and headed back down to the lower levels where she knew she would be in the company of other members of the Mansion staff...and less likely to be harassed by the curious antics of the resident specter.

As previously mentioned, Maria is no stranger to the ghostly goings-on in and around the Mansion. During the many years she has worked there, Maria has had more than her fair share of paranormal experiences. She told me she did not welcome the activity and preferred to not be alone in certain areas of the house, especially the second floor. During my conversation with Maria, she said that although the strange activity in the Mansion was not limited to the second floor, it was on that level that she has witnessed the majority of the location's unexplained phenomena. It is also on this level where several other members of the Mansion staff have experienced strange phenomena, some subtle in nature, and some quite disturbing.

Sometime during the Governor Allen administration, 1994 to 1998, Maria was working on the second floor and had a puzzling experience that was also shared by Tutti. Maria had been working close to one of the Governor's children's bedrooms and had heard the faint whining sound of a toy remote-control car moving around under one of the children's beds. Curious, Maria entered the bedroom and looked under the bed, and sure enough there was a small remote-control toy car with its wheels spinning. In order to conserve the batteries, Maria located the toy's power switch, turned it off, and left the room.

Several minutes after leaving the child's room, Maria was surprised to again hear the whining of the remote-control toy car's electric motor running beneath the bed. Maria again entered the bedroom and looked under the bed, but as she looked, the motor immediately stopped. Puzzled, Maria simply assumed that there was some sort of short-circuit in the toy's electronics that was responsible for its strange behavior and again left the room, returning to her work. But, as she walked down the hallway away from the bedroom, the distinct sound of the toy car's electric motor running beneath the bed could again be heard. At this point, she summoned Tutti.

Maria explained to Tutti what was going on with the toy car, and the fact that she had switched it off, yet continued to hear it running. Intrigued, Tutti immediately went to the room and located the still-running toy car. Only, this time, Tutti picked up the car and removed its batteries, leaving the toy lifeless beneath the bed. Now satisfied that the problem had been solved, both he and Maria left the room. However, as they walked down the hallway, they were shocked to again hear the sound of the toy car's electric motor. They knew that the batteries had been removed and there was no way the toy car should be running, but, being quite used to the frequent strange and unexplained activity within the Mansion, they decided to simply leave well enough alone and carry on with other duties.

Ghostly Whispers

Another more personal ghostly encounter that Maria experienced within the Mansion, and one that I'm sure she'll never forget, took place during the last days of the Governor Allen administration. Maria was in one of the Mansion's second-floor bathrooms, hanging a new shower curtain in preparation for the anticipated arrival of the newly elected Governor Gilmore and his family. She was the only person in the Mansion at the time and had come in early that morning to prepare for the new First Family's arrival.

At around five-thirty in the morning, while in the process of hanging the new shower curtain, Maria heard from behind her a distinct voice whispering her name. Startled, but assuming the strange voice was simply Tutti playing around, Maria turned and yelled, "hello." Hearing no response, Maria again assumed Tutti had entered the Mansion and was joking around, and resumed hanging the shower curtain. Just then, she again heard the strange voice clearly say her name, as if trying to get her attention. Maria once more turned around and yelled for Tutti, but this time she ventured into the hallway outside the bathroom expecting to see Tutti standing there. To her amazement, there was no one there, and she began to sense that something unusual was at play.

At this point, in an effort to rule out a practical joker, namely Tutti, Maria called down to the Mansion Gate guard shack and asked the

Capitol Police officer if Tutti or anyone else had entered the residence. The officer assured Maria that no one had entered the Mansion and she was still the only person in the residence at the time. This answer was not what Maria had wanted to hear and she now began to get a little nervous as to the possibilities of who or what had attempted to get her attention. Still, in an effort to complete her task, Maria reluctantly returned to the bathroom and resumed hanging the curtain.

Back inside the bathroom, Maria was reaching up over the bathtub, attaching the last of the curtain, when she heard her name spoken again—although, this time it was both clearer and louder, and sounded like it was spoken from right behind her. Instantly startled and in a sudden instinctual effort to flee from the room, Maria accidentally stumbled and fell into the empty bathtub, dragging the shower-curtain with her and tearing it from the rail. In a state of panic, she managed to lift herself from the bathtub and flee the bathroom, running all the way down the hallway and descending the stairs to the front door. Only after reaching the front door was Maria able to stop running and regain her composure.

Moments later, Maria observed Tutti arriving at the Mansion. Thankful that someone else was now inside the residence with her, Maria immediately went to Tutti and detailed the terrifying ordeal that had moments ago transpired on the second floor. Tutti helped Maria calm down and eventually accompanied her to the second floor to fix the shower curtain. Although Maria completed the task, months later she still remained too disturbed by the event to venture alone onto the second floor.

To this day, Maria still avoids being alone in certain areas of the Mansion. She explained to me that she quite often senses the presence of the supernatural while working alone within the residence. One of the places where she most strongly senses an eerie presence is on the second floor, directly below the attic area. Maria says that she often feels as if someone is following her every move throughout the second floor from the attic above. She described it as an intense and uncomfortable feeling that leaves her wanting to immediately leave the area.

Maria even experiences the feeling when there are other people present on the same floor. However, she is not the only person to sense this intense feeling of being watched, as other people, including one of the Mansion's maintenance staff, have reported the phenomena, too. In fact, one maintenance employee, Dave, who was one day alone changing a light bulb in the attic, came down the attic stairs and refused to go back up alone. He simply stated that, while up there, he was overcome with the sense that someone was watching him, and it had made him feel so uncomfortable that he had to leave the attic. Although other members of the Mansion staff are uncomfortable experiencing strange phenomena throughout the residence, their experiences reassure Maria that what she is feeling is real—and not just a figment of her imagination.

A Malevolent Spirit?

Many of the events experienced by Maria and others in the Mansion are considered classic examples of paranormal activity. Some of it even appears to be focused at garnering the attention of particular people. So, could it be that a ghostly entity can become familiar with, or prefer, certain individuals?

Maybe it's the frequency of a certain person's presence in a haunted place that causes an entity to focus its attention on them. Who knows? But what could be surmised from these incidents is that a lot of the haunting is not simply residual in nature, but seemingly focused and intelligent interaction. It appears obvious that whatever is responsible for the haunting of the Governor's Mansion has intentionally made contact with the living, sometimes even displaying a sense of humor with oftentimes playful phenomena. On other occasions, though, the ghost's activities seem more sinister and can be frightening, possibly the result of a more malevolent spirit.

Several months ago, another member of the Mansion's housekeeping staff was alone on the second floor vacuuming the carpets. The young woman had been upstairs for quite a while and was finishing the carpet in one of the hallways, when she felt the power cord suddenly become taut. Assuming that the excess cord had simply gotten caught under or around a piece of furniture, she forcefully tugged on the cord in an attempt to free it, but the cord did not break free. So, she switched it off and looked to see what the power cord was hooked on. However, when she looked at the cord, she could clearly see that the excess cord was coiled loosely on the floor behind her, free from obstruction.

Confused, the housekeeper grasped the cord and deliberately pulled on it. Her confusion quickly turned to fright as she felt the unmistakable sensation of someone else forcefully tugging back on the power cord. As she had picked up the excess cord from the floor and yanked on it, she had observed and felt the cord pull back as if being tugged on by an invisible entity. In fact, the tug was so forceful that the power cord was yanked clean from the young woman's hands and it fell to the floor.

Now frozen with fear, the housekeeper stood staring at the lifeless power cord when, all of a sudden, the second-floor lights went out and she was instantly plunged into darkness. At this point, she let out a blood-curdling scream and ran down the stairs to the first floor. Maria, as well as several other staff members, heard the scream and thought something terrible had happened and quickly went to her aid. Finding her on the first floor in an obvious state of panic, the staff members were shocked as the young woman related to them the details of her frightening ordeal. The lights had only remained out for several seconds, but, coupled with the terrifying tug-of-war with the invisible entity, the housekeeper was no way going back upstairs. In fact, Maria stated that she felt the woman would *never* return to the Mansion after such an unnerving experience. She eventually *did* return, but not back to the second floor—at least, not alone.

Another event that suggests the presence of a malevolent spirit haunting the Governor's Mansion is an unsettling experience that was witnessed by Maria and another member of the staff, Cynthia. The activity occurred during the last months of Governor Allen's administration while Maria and Cynthia were in the basement level of the residence, preparing for a formal dinner that was being hosted by the Governor and the First Lady.

It was sometime during the day, and Maria and others within the Mansion were busy preparing for the occasion. Maria was standing talking with Cynthia in the kitchen area of the basement when both of their attentions were suddenly drawn to the ice machine. Both women had noticed a sudden unusual movement from within the open compartment of the ice machine and had simultaneously turned to look as an aluminum ice scoop hurtled from the machine and flew across the kitchen. Stunned, they both watched as the scoop crashed noisily against the far wall of the kitchen, bounced off, and landed heavily on the floor. They were absolutely shocked. They both knew what they had just seen, but couldn't rationalize in their minds how an aluminum ice scoop could fly ten to twenty feet across a room without having been touched by anyone. There was no one in the area of the ice machine, including Maria and Cynthia, when the scoop had flown out, seemingly propelled by some unseen force. Whatever it was, the women were quite sure that it was not a natural occurrence that had thrown the scoop across the room, and both were easily convinced that what they had just witnessed was the poltergeist-like activity of the Mansion ghost—and it had definitely gotten their attention.

Yet again, the Mansion ghost apparently displayed a degree of anger or malevolence, by throwing a solid object across a room. I don't believe this behavior is simply playful in nature, as it possesses the potential for bodily harm. Obviously, the entity has used other less harmful methods in the past to garner the attention of the living, so why would it, on this occasion, choose to hurtle an aluminum ice scoop with enough force to cause it to bounce off a wall? Whatever the reason, I believe that there may indeed be more than one entity haunting the Governor's Mansion—and one with less than amicable intentions.

Moving Furniture

As previously discussed, it appears that whatever entity haunts the Governor's Mansion has the propensity to move solid objects (sometimes thought to be *poltergeist* activity), such as ice scoops, power-cords, and power switches—but, how *large* of an object a paranormal entity can potentially move is anyone's guess. Although, an incident that occurred a few years ago, experienced by Virginia Capitol Police Officer John Nicholson, indicates that the entity may possess the ability to move objects that are substantially larger than an ice scoop—objects such as living-room furniture.

As a four-and-half-year veteran of the Virginia Capitol Police, John has worked many a night within the Governor's Mansion without any noticeable incidents. But, John recently informed me of the mysterious activity he experienced, approximately three years ago, which makes him believe that whatever haunts the Mansion has the ability to move more than just ice scoops.

It was around three o'clock in the morning and John had been sitting in an office in the basement of the Mansion. The First Family was in their resident quarters on this particular occasion, but as far as John knew, they were all sound asleep, and the interior of the residence was completely quiet. John had been sitting alone in the office for quite some time and was becoming acclimated to the peaceful atmosphere when he was suddenly disturbed by the sound of heavy furniture being dragged across the floor of the room above. Assuming that there was simply another officer or member of the First Family moving something around the room, John grabbed his flashlight and made his way to the darkened first floor.

The room that sits directly above the office where John had been sitting is the Mansion's historically restored and preserved Old Governor's Office. This small room formerly served as the Governor's office before the Governor was afforded office space in the Capitol Building and is furnished with antique furniture and fittings intended to reflect how the room originally looked 200 years ago.

As John reached the first floor, he turned on his flashlight and made his way to the area where he was sure the noises had originated from. The room was, of course, dark, and he could locate no sign of anyone having been in the room, nor any sign of the heavy antique furniture having been moved. However, while standing alone within the Old Governor's Office, the interior illuminated by only the faint glow of his flashlight, John recalls sensing an unusual chill in the air that caused the hairs on his neck to stand on end, and the unmistakable feeling that he was being observed. So, bemused by the lack of any rational explanation for the noises he had heard, and now feeling quite uncomfortable standing alone in the small room, John expanded his search to include the entire first floor, but again could locate no sign of anyone having been moving around within any of the rooms.

After completing a thorough search of the first floor, John retreated back to the basement. Sitting down in the chair that he had been sitting in before he was mysteriously disturbed by the strange sounds from above, John pondered what he had experienced and hoped that what he suspected was responsible for

The historically restored Old Governor's Office
where furniture has been heard moving across
the floor in the middle of the night.
Photo by author

the noises had ceased its activity for the remainder of the night.
But, once again, John heard the same exact noises, sounding like
heavy furniture being dragged across the carpeted floor above.
Only this time, he decided to forego an investigation of the noises,
knowing quite well that whatever he suspected was responsible for
the activity was probably better left alone.

Mysterious Orbs

On the same day I spoke with Officer John Nicholson about his strange incident, I had been down at Capitol Square, accompanied by my wife and daughter, taking numerous pictures for this book. It was a cold November day in 2009, and we began inside the Capitol Building where I took detailed pictures of the interior of the building, focusing on the particular points of interest mentioned within the pages of this book. We eventually made our way to the Governor's Mansion and participated in a guided tour of the interior of the residence, during which I discussed several ghost stories with the tour guide.

The tour guide was only too pleased to share her stories with us and seemed genuinely intrigued by the couple of personal ghostly experiences I related to her.

As I had done in the Capitol Building, I took numerous photos with my digital camera of particular points of interest within the residence. I took as many photos as I could without presenting myself as a potential security threat. Suspecting that it was not entirely unfeasible that I could inadvertently capture some sort of anomaly or paranormal phenomena on camera, I chose to take a lot of pictures. I took multiple pictures from each position in order to rule out light anomalies, dirt on the lens, or any other technical issue related to the camera itself that could possibly create an image in the photos that could later be misinterpreted as paranormal activity. I was also careful not to capture the shadows of the tour guide or my wife and young daughter as they also walked around within the residence. So, camera in hand, I snapped picture after picture like any other tourist visiting the Mansion.

Upon later inspection of the photos on my PC, I was surprised to notice that on two of the photos, I appear to have captured the images of several orbs. The photos were taken in two different rooms on the first floor of the Mansion. The first picture that appears to have captured an orb was coincidentally taken in the Old Governor's Office, where Officer John Nicholson had reported hearing strange noises late one night, like heavy furniture being dragged across the floor. The two orbs can be easily seen in the picture: one, about the size of a tennis ball, apparently floating at the back of the leather chair in the right of the room, and another, approximately the same size, appearing several inches off the floor in front of a small wooden chair

Another photo of the Old Governors Office, but this one showing two distinct orbs: one floating at the rear of the leather chair to the right of the photo, the other at the top of the right leg of the small wooden chair in front of the window in the center of the picture. *Photo by author*

In this photo of the lounge room adjacent to the dining room, an orb can be clearly seen hovering above the left side of the crystal chandelier. *Photo by author*

positioned to the left of the window located in the center of the picture. The second picture was taken in a lounge-room that adjoins the dining room, and contains an old antique piano and several antique pieces of furniture. The orb, appearing to be approximately the same size as a grapefruit, can be seen slightly to the left of the large chandelier that graces the center of the room.

As discussed earlier, orbs are considered by many paranormal experts to be a form of concentrated paranormal energy that manifests itself as small spheres of light. These spheres of light are usually invisible to the naked human eye, but appear to be capable of being captured on film or by digital camera. Sometimes they appear to be hovering stationary and other times moving fast, and often they even appear to change direction as they move. Many people are skeptical of these so-called orbs, explaining them as normal, everyday light anomalies or simply dust or bugs in the air. But, others believe they hold some degree of scientific precedence that could one day unlock the mystery surrounding alleged hauntings.

I personally am a little skeptical of the orb phenomena. I agree that there are plenty of rational explanations that could easily account for the majority of photographed orbs. Some orbs, though, are simply too strange to explain without considering the possibility that they are indeed some sort of paranormal phenomena. I mean, how does anyone know for sure and, without keeping an open mind, how are we ever supposed to explore the supernatural? So, it is with a degree of skepticism that I have included the *orb* pictures for you to view, but I also accept that they *could* quite possibly be some sort of paranormal phenomena.

I'll leave it for you to make up your own mind as to their true identity. I can promise you that I did not experience anything remotely strange while I was taking the pictures, nothing was deliberately manipulated in order to create the effects, and the orbs only appear in those two photos, and not in any of the several other photos that were taken in the exact same location, from the exact same position, and under the exact same conditions.

A Final Chapter Note

On a final note to this chapter on the Governor's Mansion, I feel it's relevant to again mention that the many paranormal events reported to have occurred within the residence suggest that there may well be more than one restless spirit haunting the location. The many detailed witness reports of ghost sightings and poltergeist activity in and around the residence indicate that there may quite possibly be two or three distinctly different entities; one a young woman in a white dress, another an older gentleman dressed as a butler, and even possibly the restless spirit of a murder victim. But which one is responsible for the malevolent activity remains a mystery. Is it possible that different people illicit different behavior from certain entities? Maybe the housekeeper's mere presence on the second floor was enough to attract the attention of a malevolent entity that chose to scare her with its frightening behavior. There are numerous possibilities, but they all remind us that the paranormal is very unpredictable, should be treated with the utmost respect, and most certainly should never be deliberately provoked.

The original dining
room has hosted
many dignitaries and
historical figures
during its long tenure
and may now also play
host to the paranormal.
Photo by author

Chapter 5

The Virginia Supreme Court Building

During my first few months working for the Virginia Capitol Police, the Supreme Court Building became like a home away from home. During a regular five-night work week, I was probably assigned to the Supreme Court Building at least three out of the five nights. Therefore, I became very familiar with the location's interior, including its sub-basement levels that still house the money vaults, safes, and bullet-proof guard turrets that were installed during the building's previous tenure as Richmond's U.S. Federal Reserve Bank.

When it comes to creepy destinations, I rank the Virginia Supreme Court Building amongst the creepiest. During my time with the Virginia Capitol Police, hardly a week would go by without someone reportedly experiencing unexplained phenomena within the centuries-old building. Most of the activity was reported to be either in the sub-basement levels, or on the sixth floor, so it became commonplace for some officers to deliberately avoid these levels during their nightly patrols of the building. And, eight hours during the darkness of night is a long and lonely time to be locked inside a building that possesses such a chilling reputation for paranormal activity.

Laying basis to the claims of ghostly goings-on in the sub-basement level of the building is the story of a killing that occurred in February 1972, while the building served as the Federal Reserve Bank. The tragic killing of a bank security officer resulted from a disgruntled member of the bank's guard force going berserk with a gun. The ensuing gunfight ended with several security officers being shot by

Located adjacent to Capitol Square, the Virginia Supreme Court building once served as the Federal Reserve Bank and witnessed a tragic event that left a guard dead. *Photo by author*

the deranged man, with one reportedly dying at the scene. It is not clear from old newspaper reports if the guard who initiated the violent confrontation is the person who was killed, but I'm sure that whoever did die from the gunshots experienced a rather unexpected and untimely death, a factor considered by many paranormal experts to be a major precursor to classic haunting cases.

To this day, the evidence of the gun battle still remains in the sub-basement of the building. Several of the reinforced guard turrets display bullet holes in their thick glass and steel, and a couple of other holes can be found in the surrounding concrete walls, providing a chilling reminder of the events that occurred during that fateful day in 1972.

A Chilling Encounter

Several months into my service as a Capitol Police officer, I found myself once more on graveyard shift duty in the Supreme Court Building. It was a weekend, and the premises had been closed for business since Friday evening. The only people who had been in the building since Friday were the cleaning crew and members of the Capitol Police. On that particular night, I was again alone within its walls for another long and lonely eight hours.

As usual, I began my shift by double-checking all of the exterior doors and the security system. I then made my way to the sixth floor, where, in the kitchen area, I switched on the coffee maker and made a fresh pot of coffee. Located opposite the elevators, the kitchen was the only one in the building and was equipped as a break-room for the numerous state employees who worked at the Supreme Court during the day, and contained seating, vending machines, a microwave oven, and various other break-room fixtures.

For me, the kitchen provided not only a place to acquire a fresh cup of coffee, but its well-lit and modern decor also offered a reprieve from the rest of the building's age-old and traditional interior design. Walking through certain sections of the building was like traveling through a time warp, as modern design and color contrasted the much older-looking motifs and colors of the courtrooms, chambers, and judicial offices. In places, the building truly showed its age.

After starting a fresh pot of coffee, I began my patrol of the sixth floor. Much like the mundane job of a security officer, Capitol Police officers were required to perform regular checks of the interior of buildings they were assigned to, so I was ready to walk every dimly lit corridor of the building, checking every floor and every door.

Leaving the kitchen area of the sixth floor and proceeding past the freight elevator, the corridor suddenly narrows and leads into the older-looking part of the building. Many of the lights in this area are turned off at night, so it is always good practice to have a flashlight handy to lead the way. The maze of corridors and hallways within the building can be confusing and it takes several nights to learn the building's layout, which stretches the entire width of a city block.

Past the freight elevator and entering the older portion of the sixth floor level, all of a sudden, I noticed something move about thirty feet in front of me. I did not have my flashlight on at the time, but something moving in the dimly lit corridor directly ahead of me definitely caught my attention. Not sure as to what it was, I stopped and stared straight ahead. There was not enough illumination from behind me to cast my shadow so far up the corridor, nor was there a window or open door close by that could facilitate a moving shadow.

I didn't see the shadow long enough to describe it with any detail, but it was definitely a dark mass that appeared to quickly dart from one side of the corridor to the other, from right to left. Momentarily startled, I stopped walking and stood still, listening for the sounds of anyone moving up ahead. As I stood still, my senses now alerting to the presence of something out of the ordinary, I suddenly detected a strong whiff of cigar smoke...not so strange, considering that some of the building's employees still smoked in their offices, but strange enough considering there was no one other than me in the building at the time.

The air was still, as I stood in the middle of the corridor, but I noticed a cold draft gently pass by me as I began to walk towards the area where I had observed the moving shadow. The reason I noticed the draft was because it was unusually cold, in fact, quite chillingly cold, and I began to shiver. But again, trying to find a rational explanation for what I was experiencing, I reasoned that the unusually cold air was likely produced by the building's air-conditioning, even though it was wintertime and the air-conditioning was most certainly turned off.

I continued slowly towards the end of the corridor and, as I did, the odor of cigar smoke became increasingly present. At this point, I assumed that there was possibly someone in one of the many adjoining offices who was smoking a cigar, and I called out to whoever was there. Receiving no response, I called out again and, as I did, I experienced one of the most intense and unnerving feelings of paranormal presence I have ever felt. I can only describe it as a chillingly cold static electric charge that engulfed my entire body, causing every hair on my body to instantly stand on end. My heart skipped a beat and I was overcome with the overwhelming desire to immediately leave the area. The odor of cigar smoke was so intense that it almost seemed like someone had blown the smoke directly into my face, but there was no smoke visible, nor was there anyone else around. All I knew was that I felt that I was most definitely not alone in that area and it would be in my best interest to postpone my progress down that particular corridor. I turned and walked hastily back towards the elevator, while suppressing the urge to break into a run.

Once back in the comforting light of the kitchen area, I managed to regain my composure and persuaded myself to venture back down the eerie corridor again. I convinced myself that whatever I had experienced there could not hurt me and it was my duty to continue my rounds of the building. So, after a couple of minutes in the kitchen, I walked cautiously back to the area where I had just experienced what I strongly suspect was a paranormal presence. Only, when I reached the place of my strange encounter, the atmosphere had completely changed. There was no longer any odor of cigar smoke, nor did I experience anything resembling the unnerving sensations I had felt moments before. The temperature now felt normal, and I did not sense any fear or hesitation at continuing down the corridor. But, as a duty-bound precaution, I decided to check the interior of the offices in close proximity to verify that there was no one present and no cigar accidentally left burning in an ashtray.

I checked all the offices in the immediate area, but could not locate anyone. I also could no longer detect any trace of an odor of cigar smoke. The whole scenario just seemed completely strange. Surely, after noticing such an intense aroma of a burning cigar, there would remain at least some trace of the scent for several minutes, but that was not the case. After sensing the presence of whatever it was that had been with me in the corridor, I could not believe that it had dissipated so quickly.

I later considered that the experience may have resulted from actually passing by an invisible ghostly entity as it too walked down the corridor. Whatever it was, it left a lasting memory with me. Never before had I experienced such an intensely unnerving feeling that I was in the presence of something paranormal, nor have I ever since. And, although I would only experience on one more occasion evidence of a paranormal presence in the Supreme Court Building, what happened to one of my colleagues several months later on that same floor left me glad that I did not come face-to-face with whatever may have passed by me that night.

A Menacing Apparition

One of the most chilling and memorable paranormal experiences that I believe has ever occurred inside the Supreme Court Building happened to a young lady (who we'll call Emma, as she wishes her true identity to remain anonymous), who worked for several years as a security officer for the Virginia Capitol Police.

The incident occurred late one night, in 2003, during the graveyard shift, as Emma was patrolling the interior of the Supreme Court Building. At the time, I was on duty at another location within the Capitol Complex and heard the frightening events unfold over the police radio. I later spoke with Emma about the events and she recalled to me in detail the terrifying ordeal that caused her to flee the building and consider quitting her job.

Emma had been on duty in the Supreme Court Building for several hours, as she had on numerous other graveyard shifts during her time serving with the Virginia Capitol Police, and was patrolling the lonely hallways of the sixth floor. Emma had worked the graveyard shift at the Supreme Court so often that she knew its rooms and corridors like the back of her hand and was unfazed by rumors of the building's ghostly reputation. Having worked within the aging building so many times, Emma had developed a routine to her patrols and would often stop at the sixth-floor kitchen to grab a snack from one of the vending machines. And on this night, she did just that.

Standing facing the glass front of the vending machine, Emma began retrieving the change from her pocket. As she looked down, counting the change in her hands, Emma was confident that there was no one else in the building and so was a little surprised to see the reflection of a person other than her in the glass, slowly approaching her from behind. Immediately looking up at the unexpected company, Emma was suddenly struck with an intense sense of terror that froze her to the very spot she was standing—for, standing behind her, reflected in the glass, was the image of what she later described as a tall menacing-looking, bearded man with dark, curly hair, wearing an aged, brown suit.

Frozen with fear, Emma was absolutely convinced of what she was seeing. Her senses told her that this was not a real person standing only inches behind her, with his head tilted forward, facing the floor, but with his eyes looking up and directly at hers in the reflection in the glass. The sudden shock of the encounter caused her to drop the change from her hands, but, unable to move, she was forced to observe the ghostly apparition for several long seconds before the sheer terror of the moment released its paralyzing grip and she was able to flee from the kitchen.

Escaping the kitchen and the menacing apparition within, Emma ran across the hallway to the elevator, but after frantically pressing the buttons in her now hysterical state, she decided that the elevator was too slow and instead fled to the stairs. It took her little time to descend the six floors of stairs and, reaching the lobby level, she ran from the building and out onto the sidewalk, where she frantically called on her radio for assistance.

Hearing her hysterical tone on the radio, every officer listened intently as the events unfolded and two Capitol Police officers were dispatched to Emma's aid. It was quite clear that something had truly terrified Emma and had caused her to flee the building, but exactly what had happened was unclear until Emma had calmed down enough to recall the terrifying details.

Recounting the events to the responding officers, and later to me, she recalled how she had observed the reflection of the apparition standing behind her, but when she had finally been able to turn and run from the kitchen, expecting to see the menacing entity standing before her, there had been no one standing there. She further stated that the spectral image looked so real that she clearly remembered that it appeared to be an older man with thick, scruffy, curly, brown hair, a short, thick beard, and wearing a brown suit. He had appeared several inches taller than her and although facing down towards the ground, the ghostly apparition's eyes were staring up forebodingly into the reflection of her own eyes as she stood before the glass face of the vending machine. Almost as if to compound her terror, the ghost then had either lightly touched or blown on the back of Emma's neck, as she definitely recalled feeling an intense icy-cold sensation a moment before she was able to flee the location.

Emma was so terrified by her ordeal that she refused to re-enter the building. The two Capitol Police officers who had responded to her aid performed a thorough check of the interior of the premises, but were unable to locate anyone. The security system had not alerted to the presence of anyone else in the building, and there again appeared to be no rational explanation for the disturbing event. Whatever it was that terrified Emma that night, it had such an effect on her that, at her request, she was permanently reassigned to work at another location.

From this event, a couple of questions are raised. Why did the entity choose to appear to Emma on that particular night? Emma had been working in that building for years without ever witnessing any significant unexplained phenomena, as had many other officers. So why did the entity choose her? It had quite obviously made its presence known to me, as well as several other reliable witnesses, but had never actually manifested itself into a visible human form. Whatever the reason, this incident was not the entity's last reported manifestation, as it appeared to make its presence known to another officer several months later at that same location.

The Resident Phantom

Officer Gonzales (not his real name) was a police officer for the Virginia Capitol Police during the same period I served. I remember speaking to Gonzales about this following incident a few days after it occurred. Intrigued by the paranormal, I was always interested to hear the details of ghostly encounters from the people who experienced them firsthand and within the ranks of the Virginia Capitol Police, there never seemed to be a shortage of credible witnesses to paranormal events.

Like all officers, Gonzales pulled his fair share of graveyard shifts in the Supreme Court Building and, like most other officers, he was aware of the building's reputation for unexplained phenomena. But, Gonzales's experience in the Supreme Court Building in 2004 goes down as one of the most curious experiences in the history of the Virginia Capitol Police.

It was just after midnight and Officer Gonzales was working alone in the Supreme Court Building, as he did several nights per week. On this particular night, Gonzales was completing his patrol of the building's interior, checking the exterior doors and ensuring that the building was indeed secure. As usual, the interior of the building was in its typical evening state of limited illumination, as only the most necessary lights remained on. Gonzales had checked the basement and sub-basement levels without incident and had made his way through

The entrance to the 8th Street side of the
Supreme Court building. Beyond these
doors, several Capitol Police officers
have witnessed the location's ghostly
inhabitant. *Photo by author*

the building's multiple levels of long corridors and hallways until he
reached the elevator and ascended to the sixth floor.

As the elevator doors slowly opened and Gonzales stepped off into
the corridor, he was passed by a gentleman he didn't immediately
recognize, but due to the person's obvious casual demeanor, Gonzales
assumed he was an employee working late, not an unusual occurrence
in that particular area of the building. But, as Gonzales walked several

steps past the man, he suddenly realized that he did not observe his identification badge, something that was required to be displayed at all times within the building.

Turning around, Gonzales observed the gentleman, now a little ways down the corridor, and called out to him to get his attention. The man continued to walk on as if ignoring the officer, so Gonzales picked up his pace and quickly attempted to catch up with him. As he pursued the man, Gonzales again politely requested him to stop, but to no avail. After several more paces, Gonzales increased to a jog in order to catch up with the man. By this point, it was clear to Gonzales that the person had no intention of complying with his request, so he yelled for the man to stop. Again, though, the person casually proceeded on his way as if not even aware of the officer's presence.

Just as Officer Gonzales was about to catch up to him, the person turned the corner to a connecting hallway and disappeared from view. Now only a few feet behind the person, Gonzales also turned the corner, but to his shock and surprise, the mystery man had simply disappeared.

A little confused as to where the gentleman could have gone, Gonzales continued down the hallway in search of him. Checking the adjoining offices and continuing to the very end of the hallway in an attempt to locate anyone who may have been on the sixth floor, Gonzales made a concerted effort at finding a rational explanation for what he had just observed. While realizing there was absolutely no possibility that a person could simply have disappeared, Gonzales also realized that a larger search of the building would be required to ensure the integrity of the building's security.

Shortly after, Officer Gonzales summoned several other officers in an effort to conduct a thorough search of the area. The search took the officers quite a while, but they were unable to locate anyone else in the building. Concluding their search, the officers gathered in a corridor to discuss the incident. Suspecting that his integrity may be in question, Gonzales assured his colleagues that he was not losing his mind and that he was not seeing things. He even gave a detailed description of the person he had seen as he exited the elevator, describing him as a middle-aged gentleman with dark hair and a beard, wearing a dark suit and tie. But, confident that there was no one hiding in the building, the officers turned and began to leave.

As the officers walked together towards the elevators, Officer Gonzales noticed a picture on the wall that he instantly recognized as the mystery gentleman he had moments earlier observed on the sixth floor. He immediately notified his colleagues of the discovery and watched as they each viewed the picture. Upon close inspection, it quickly became evident to the other officers that the person in the picture, although formerly a long-time employee of the Supreme Court, had died several years earlier.

Gonzales watched as the expressions on his colleagues' faces changed to a look of bewilderment, as they informed him of the fact that the mystery person he had just identified had passed away years before. Suspecting that Gonzales was mistaken in his identification of the person in the picture, they began poking fun at him. Gonzales swore that the person in the picture was definitely the person he had earlier encountered on the sixth floor. He too was confused by the scenario, but he was also confident in his own sanity and was convinced that he had correctly identified the mystery person.

The more Gonzales accepted that what he had witnessed could possibly have been a ghost, the more the circumstances appeared to support the theory. Gonzales knew that there was no way that a person could simply have disappeared right in front of him, and he also knew that he had been no more than ten feet behind him when the person had turned the corner and vanished. But what disturbed Gonzales even more was the fact that the description of the ghostly entity was strikingly similar to that which had been reported several months earlier by Emma. Gonzales now believed it possible that, like Emma, he had in fact experienced the Supreme Court's resident phantom.

Noisy Spirit

Most of the time, working the Supreme Court during the long and lonely nighttime hours proved uneventful, but every so often I was reminded of its eerie reputation. One night in particular, I was seated at the security desk located just inside the Eighth Street entrance of the building, reading a magazine, when I experienced what I believe was the ghost's attempt at making its presence known.

Located several feet from the security desk was a concrete-floored corridor leading around to the left where one of the building's several

Leading to one of the courtrooms, this narrow corridor once echoed the crashing sound of the old brass "Quiet" sign hitting the stone floor. The old sign has since been replaced by the newer lighter one seen in the picture, but stood in exactly the same place. *Photo by author*

large courtrooms was located. Standing just outside the courtroom's large wooden doors, between the thick stone walls of the hallway, was an aluminum sign atop a four-foot brass post that read: "Quiet Please, Court in Session." This sign had been standing for years outside of the courtroom and was rarely moved due to the weight of its stand. After accidentally knocking into it several times with my equipment bag as I passed by it on my way to the security desk, I found that it would not easily fall.

I had been sitting at the desk for several minutes after completing yet another patrol of the building's interior, when I was suddenly jolted to my senses by the sound of the heavy brass-posted sign falling onto the concrete floor. It was around two o'clock in the morning and I knew that no one else was on the premises, so the sound made me jump, as it loudly and unexpectedly shattered the building's peaceful nighttime atmosphere.

At the sound of the loud crash, I immediately jumped up and walked around the corner of the corridor, expecting to see one of my colleagues picking up the sign. To my shock and surprise, though, there was no one there and the sign was standing up straight, appearing to have never been moved. If anyone had entered the building, the security system would have alerted me to the fact and I would have noticed them on the security cameras. So, I was confused as to how I had definitely heard the distinct sound of the sign hitting the corridor's concrete floor when there appeared to be no logical reason for it having done so. The sound had been so loud that it echoed throughout the building's concrete walls and had jolted me from my relaxed state as I sat reading at the desk, to my now acutely alert, and somewhat bemused, state of mind.

For a minute, I stood in the corridor staring at the sign. I could not believe what I had just heard and I refused to believe that it was merely my senses deceiving me. I was convinced that the sign had definitely fallen to the floor, but there was simply no way that anyone could have knocked it over, picked it back up, and fled the area undetected. I only had to walk twenty feet or so to the corner of the corridor where I could observe the sign at the entrance of the courtroom, so there was just no way.

After a minute or two of examining the sign, I checked the immediate area, the interior of the courtroom, and the full length of the corridor leading to the other side of the building, and could not locate anyone or anything that could rationally explain the incident. The only thing I could detect was the familiar uneasy sensation that I had felt before within the location. After the terrifying ordeal that Emma had recently experienced, I was not too excited about the possibility of meeting whatever entity was responsible for this particularly unnerving incident.

Fortunately, I never met the building's resident phantom on that particular night, and the remainder of the shift passed without incident. In fact, other than the odd unexplained sound, cold spot, or the acute sense of not being alone, the rest of my shifts at the Supreme Court Building also passed without witnessing any significant paranormal phenomena. However, that's not to say that other people did not witness ghostly activity within the premises, as conversations with several of my colleagues would later reveal.

"Creeped Out!"

Another officer who experienced strange phenomena within the Supreme Court Building is Officer Jose DeJesus. Jose served with the Virginia Capitol Police from 2004 to 2008 and, like most of the other officers, spent his fair share of graveyard shifts patrolling the interior of many of the Capitol's historic buildings. It was on one such occasion, while alone inside the Supreme Court, that Jose first experienced what he believes to be the location's resident spirit.

The incident occurred one night during the early hours of the morning, while Jose was performing his initial checks of the premises. Having recently completed his field-training, this was to be Jose's first night performing his duties alone inside the building. At around one o'clock in the morning, Jose was on the sixth floor and had stopped in one of the dimly lit hallways to take a closer look at some pictures and literature that were posted along the wall. The location was of course unoccupied at the time, but as Jose stood alone in the hallway he suddenly became keenly aware that someone was standing directly behind him. He turned to look, but there was no one there. He turned back around and resumed his reading, but as he continued to read, the uncomfortable feeling became increasingly intense to the point where he was convinced that someone, or something, really was standing behind him, watching him as he looked at the pictures on the wall. In fact, Jose recalled that the sensation made him feel a little "creeped out!"

Becoming increasingly creeped out and now sensing an unusually cold chill in the air, Jose decided to leave the immediate area and retreat to a more comfortable location, such as the first floor. As he walked down the corridor, Jose remembers that the atmosphere suddenly changed and the uneasy feeling he'd endured rapidly dissipated. It was almost as if whatever had caused him to sense its presence in the hallway was seemingly localized to that one location and had not followed him. Of course, Jose could not see whatever it was that was apparently making its presence known, but the intense experience had left him with little doubt that it was present.

After checking the remainder of the premises, Jose returned to the sixth floor to face his fears and conclude his check of the building. Unlike before, though, he could no longer detect any sense that he was not alone or was being watched, nor could he detect any other evidence of the presence of the paranormal. As far as Jose recalls, the remainder of the shift proved uneventful, as no further abnormal activity occurred; at least, not to his knowledge.

Later on in his service with the Virginia Capitol Police, Jose would again experience similar paranormal activity while patrolling alone within the Capitol Building and the Governor's Mansion. Although he doesn't recall ever witnessing anything as conclusive as a full-bodied apparition, the strong sensation that Jose experienced within several of the buildings around the Capitol has left him with little doubt that the locations may indeed be haunted.

The Sub-Basement

Officer Mike Walter worked for the Virginia Capitol Police from 1996 to 1998 and has endured numerous shifts locked alone inside many of the historic buildings associated with Capitol Square. During a recent interview, Mike stated to me that he never experienced any memorable unusual activity while patrolling within the buildings of the Capitol complex, except for the Supreme Court. In fact, he recalled that the Supreme Court Building was the creepiest location he has ever worked in.

Mike explained to me that while working in the Supreme Court, he always felt uncomfortable, as though he was being watched all the time, especially while manning the guard turret located in the alley that allows access to the Supreme Court Building's basement parking lot. He stated that as he sat alone inside the cramped turret that served as an office for Capitol Police officers, he would on occasion feel that someone was standing directly behind him, watching his every move. It wasn't a noise or an icy cold chill, but just an acute awareness of another presence. Although Mike never visually observed anything out of the ordinary at that particular location, the strange feeling, which he has never experienced anywhere else

124

One of the reinforced steel
turrets that used to protect the
guards of the former Federal
Reserve Bank and now seats
officers of the Virginia Capitol
Police. *Photo by author*

since, would become so uncomfortable he would feel it necessary to leave the area.

Mike also felt intensely uncomfortable in the area of the sub-basement. Of course, the sub-basement level was the scene of the tragic shooting that left a man dead back in 1972, and is the level considered by most Capitol Police officers to be the creepiest. Mike would often stand still in the doorway of the sub-basement and stare into the darkness as he was engulfed with the inexplicable sensation that something bad was about to happen. He knew he was the only person in the building and he knew there was no one else in the sub-basement, but regardless, he still sensed the overwhelming presence of someone watching him from the dark shadows of the corridors. Being a former U.S. Marine and not afraid of the dark, Mike continued his checks of the sub-basement, constantly aware of the strange feeling, but refusing to let it unnerve him.

Although Mike admits that he never witnessed anything conclusive, he did mention that on occasions, while alone checking the area of the sub-basement level of the Supreme Court, he would observe a small strange light emitted from within the darkest areas of the rooms. Mike remembers the light appearing to be about the size of a silver dollar and would sometimes appear in the lower portions of the rooms, and other times high up towards the ceiling. Although the strange orb of light emitted a noticeable amount of seemingly fluorescent light, Mike recalls that it mysteriously did not appear to illuminate much around it, but what was even more captivating about the strange light was that even though he would attempt to follow it in an effort to reach its source, the light would always appear to fade further away.

Another location within the Supreme Court Building where Mike often experienced the uncomfortable feeling of being watched is the building's law library, which consists of a large room containing long rows of wooden bookshelves upon which thousands of thick heavy books are neatly stacked for the benefit of lawyers, law scholars, judges, and the like. The room does not differ in appearance to the stereotypical historical library where rows of tall shelves create somewhat of a maze of aisles, and where stacks and stacks of aged and dusty books adorn every inch of available space. The room also retained its own unique eerie atmosphere that seemed to be intensified by the absence of lights, which were usually off during the midnight hours.

Whatever the source of the mysterious light or the strange sensations that would overwhelm him in certain areas of the building, Mike is convinced that it was related to the location's reputed paranormal activity. Although Mike admits that he never witnessed anything that could be considered absolute proof of the presence of the paranormal, after experiencing other strange phenomena such as disembodied footsteps and banging doors, he strongly believes that the location is haunted.

On a lighter note, I have to admit that after hearing Mike's testimony regarding the uncomfortable feeling he experienced while walking alone through the library in the middle of night, I recalled experiencing a similar sensation at the same location. I had been walking through the library in the middle of the night, passing between the stacks of books, when I heard a sound that made me freeze. It was probably just the wooden shelves creaking behind me, but as I stood there alone in the darkness with only my flashlight to guide my way, I couldn't help but think of the Hollywood movie *Ghostbusters* and the opening scenes of the movie that depict an unsuspecting female librarian wandering alone through the seemingly endless rows of shelves, unaware that several books are levitating and floating freely across the passages behind her. I swear I could even recall the eerie music that accompanied the scene. Of course, remembering what the elderly librarian faced when she finally met the terrifying spectral entity responsible for the activity made me extremely hesitant to glance behind me. Fortunately, I eventually accepted the craziness of the Hollywood-fueled notion and continued on undeterred through the rows of bookshelves.

For whatever reason, it appears that ever since watching that movie when I was a child during the 1980s, I have felt uncomfortable in libraries. I know it was only a movie, but it appears some scenes leave a lasting impression on children and that one definitely creeped me out. But no matter what is responsible for the activity that appears to transpire within the Supreme Court Building, I suspect that it has nothing to do with the effect that certain Hollywood movies had on children of the '80s. I suspect that the experiences endured by the many independent witnesses to the location's strange phenomena have occurred without provocation and have displayed unique behavioral characteristics—characteristics that support the theory that the phenomena is real and not just the product of overactive imaginations influenced by the knowledge of the similar experiences of others.

Chapter 6

More Haunted Capitol Locations

Although the majority of supernatural activity said to have occurred around Capitol Square has been linked to the Capitol Building, Governor's Mansion, and the Supreme Court, there have also been numerous reports originating from other nearby locations. Strictly speaking, Capitol Square is the area of state property that surrounds the Capitol Building within the confines of the iron railing fence that lines the perimeter of the Square. Closely surrounding the property are several other buildings of interest that also belong to the Commonwealth of Virginia and have produced some equally interesting accounts of unexplained phenomena.

It may be that the reason for the apparent low number of reported paranormal events stemming from these other properties, compared to the unusually large amount of activity originating from other buildings within the Capitol complex, is that these other locations are not staffed during the nighttime hours by officers of the Capitol Police, and so any activity that occurs is far less likely to be witnessed and subsequently reported. Occasionally, there are reasons for persons to be in these other properties during the nighttime hours, such as for routine patrols, providing a prime opportunity for unsuspecting witnesses to experience whatever ghostly entities may exist within their walls.

Old City Hall

Built in 1894, the Victorian Gothic appearance of Richmond's Old City Hall, with its tall, granite walls and spires, likely lends to the building's supernatural reputation. Located on the north side of the Capitol Square, the four-story building once served as Richmond's

The architectural splendor of the Old City Hall. Standing on the north side of Capitol Square, this ominous-looking building has been the scene of at least one bizarre and unexplained incident.
Photo by author

City Hall and today provides office space for several state and private agencies.

The flamboyant architecture of the interior of the building reflects the Old City Hall's Victorian Gothic exterior and includes a three-story colorfully painted cast-iron foyer. Once saved from demolition by the Richmond Historical Society, it was designated a U.S. National Historic Landmark in 1971, and remains a prominent feature of Virginia's celebrated Capitol Square.

During my service with the Virginia Capitol Police, I heard several stories of strange occurrences within the Old City Hall, from eerie noises and lights to mysterious figures seen moving throughout the building long after it had been vacated for the evening. However, the one that most intrigues me is an account given to me by Officer Brian Alexander, a ten-year veteran of Virginia's Capitol Police.

It was during the fall of 2000, late one evening, when at around 9:30 p.m., an employee of the adjacent General Assembly Building called the Capitol Police to report several strange banging noises coming from the area within the Old City Hall. The witness stated to the responding Capitol Police officers that the noises sounded like someone possibly trying to break through the heavy wooden exterior doors of the loading area of the building.

Knowing that the building was unoccupied at that time of night, and fearing that someone was attempting to break in, Brian and four other Capitol Police officers conducted a thorough search of the dark exterior of the building, including an inspection of all exterior doorways and windows. During the search, the officers were unable to locate anyone in the area, nor signs of an attempted break-in, so they prepared to perform a check of the interior of the location as well.

As the officers stood on the concrete sidewalk discussing their plan, only a few feet from where the loud banging noises reportedly originated from, they were shocked to hear several more loud bangs emanating from within the premises. Brian described the noises as sounding like the building's large heavy wooden doors being rammed by a solid, heavy object.

At this point, the officers formulated a plan and entered the location, splitting up in order to effectively search the entire structure. It took quite a while for them to investigate every dark hallway and office of the building's aged interior, but room by room they conducted their search and checked that every exterior door was locked and that there were no signs of an attempted break-in. After a thorough search, the officers were satisfied that there was no one in the building and, after securing the exit behind them, they exited the darkened Old City Hall.

Again standing outside the building, the officers were just about to clear from the scene when the loud banging erupted once more from within the Old City Hall's thick granite walls. Convinced that there was absolutely no one inside, the officers were now increasingly curious as to the origin of the noises, and they all quickly re-entered the building and performed another search. As before, the officers could not locate anyone or anything within the location that could explain the extremely loud banging noises. After re-securing the exterior doors, the officers left the scene a little bewildered as to who or what was responsible for the strange disturbances.

There was no one inside the Old City Hall and there was nothing that could explain such loud banging noises. The noises may have continued throughout the night, but they went unreported. And so another strange occurrence was added to the Capitol Police's reporting archives labeled *Suspicious Incident*—one that very likely may have been another example of the area's unusual, unexplainable, and often bizarre activity.

Morrison Row

Opposite the rear of the Governor's Mansion, and overlooking Governor Street, stand several state-owned properties known as Morrison Row. The buildings house various state government departments, including the Division of Natural Heritage and the Commission for the Arts, and were constructed well over 100 years ago. The rear of the row of three-story buildings overlooks the back parking lot of the Old South Hospital Building, which is now part of the Department of Transportation's Headquarters and sits adjacent to Morrison Row at the top of Governor Street. Although not requiring 24-hour staffing by Capitol Police officers, being a state-owned property, the row of buildings is routinely patrolled during the nighttime hours and has, on occasion, revealed some peculiar activity.

One such occasion occurred several years ago and was witnessed by a couple of officers, including Sergeant Phil White. Phil had been conducting a routine midnight check of the property and had found one of the doors on the Governor Street side of the building unlocked, so, adhering to Capitol Police policy, Phil notified his colleagues of the discovery and proceeded to check the inside of the building.

Entering the location's dark interior, Phil's senses were immediately alerted to the presence of something unusual. Being no stranger to the area's paranormal activities, he cautiously observed his every step as he slowly proceeded to the basement level with only the glow of a flashlight to illuminate the way.

Reaching the basement level, Phil curiously looked around with his light. In the darkness, he could find no sign of anyone being in the area and he began to assume that an employee had simply forgotten to lock the door before leaving for the evening. So, not overly concerned with the dilemma, Phil turned to exit the basement. As he turned to leave, though, Phil's flashlight illuminated the lower half of the room and he noticed the strange image of several footprints on the concrete floor. Phil knew that the footprints were not his, as they led to an area where he had not yet been, but what was strange about the prints was that they looked as though they were formed by a white powdery substance—not as if someone had walked through powder already on the floor, but more like the prints themselves were formed with powder on an otherwise clean surface.

Strange as the footprints seemed, Phil was confident the building was vacant and continued towards the steps that led from the basement level. Just as he reached the bottom of the steps, Phil suddenly heard the distinct sound of footsteps climbing the stairs in the darkness ahead of him. He quickly shone his flashlight towards the area, but did not see anyone as the sounds faded towards the top of the stairs. Phil immediately followed and proceeded to the first floor in order to investigate, but upon reaching the location, he continued to hear the footsteps as they ascended the unlit stairway towards the upper levels. Of course, Phil continued his pursuit and eventually found himself standing alone in the darkness of the second floor.

Scanning the area with his light, Phil was confident that the upper floors were deserted. There were no lights on and he could easily sense that there was no one there. But, in the back of his mind Phil was also aware of the familiar feeling that something was watching him from the darkness. Still, unperturbed by the eeriness of the situation, he continued his check of the second and third levels with only his flashlight to guide the way.

After finding no sign of anyone having entered the building, Phil made his way back down the stairs to the first floor, where he was joined by another officer, Steve Robinson. Phil advised Steve of the footprints and the fact that he had heard footsteps on the stairs, but also advised him that after a thorough search of the building, he was confident that there was no one inside. Both men then made their way out of the front door and around the side of the exterior of the building.

Reaching the rear of the building, and facing away from the back door, Phil and Steve stood and discussed the incident. As it was the early hours of the morning, there was little noise as they stood chatting in the darkness. Then, all of a sudden, the quiet was interrupted by the sound of the back door of the building suddenly and violently

Situated to the rear of the Executive Mansion, the buildings of Morrison Row are said to also experience the Capitol area's paranormal activity. *Photo by author*

swinging open as if propelled by an unseen force. So forceful was the motion of the door that it banged loudly against the outer wall and almost came off its hinges. Both men were momentarily startled as they looked on in disbelief, half expecting someone to come charging out of the building. But no one appeared. Phil and Steve both immediately raced towards the open door, and after announcing the incident over the radio, entered the building. An additional officer arrived on scene within moments, her attention captured by the urgent tone of Phil's voice over the radio, and assisted Phil and Steve with another thorough search of the location's interior.

On the east side of the Capitol, the Old
Finance building classically reflects the
period architecture of Capitol Square.
Photo by author

The search of the building's interior revealed no signs of anyone
having been inside. The footprints that Phil had observed on the
floor of the basement had mysteriously disappeared and nothing else
appeared disturbed. Both men had just witnessed the door swing open
violently and knew there was no way someone could have exited the
building without being seen. They had only been several feet from the
door when it had opened, and aside from the time it took both men to
immediately turn and look, there was little opportunity for someone
to escape the premises undetected.

It was with little doubt in his mind that Phil felt the experience
had been the result of paranormal activity. There was no obvious
rational explanation for what the officers had just witnessed and,
coupled with the strange footprints that apparently disappeared as
mysteriously as they had appeared, there was enough to convince Phil
that this particular building may also play host to the supernatural.

Besides, no one ever claimed that the Capitol's ghosts were confined to the limits of the Square, and it is quite conceivable that whatever paranormal energy lingers within the area had also found its way to other nearby properties.

The General Assembly building overlooks the north-west corner of Capitol Square and today provides the offices of the Commonwealth's legislature. *Photo by author*

Conclusion

During my tenure with the Virginia Capitol Police, I believe I experienced more than my fair share of otherworldly activity and feel extremely fortunate to have done so. I don't believe any other location could have provided me with a deeper insight into the paranormal. Yes, I had ghostly experiences before serving as a police officer, but it was while working as a cop that I became truly fascinated with the supernatural, rekindling an interest that began during my childhood.

While writing this book, I had time to reminisce some of the events that I, and many others, witnessed in and around Virginia's Capitol Complex. Although exciting and sometimes quite frightening, many of the strange events and unexplained phenomena left me pondering the answers to several questions, such as:

- Why is there so much ghostly activity in and around Virginia's State Capitol?
- Why did the activity appear to occur so often?
- Why do some buildings appear to play host to strange activity and others don't?
- And, how many other witnesses are out there who haven't offered their ghostly experiences to the development of this book?

Of course, one can only wonder. As a person who merely possesses an avid interest in the paranormal, and not as a self-proclaimed *ghost hunter* or *paranormal investigator*, I can only speculate as to the answers to these questions.

The activity allegedly experienced in and around the Capitol Complex does appear to occur with startling frequency. This, I believe,

Capitol Police stand guard over the entrance to Capitol Square. During the night, these officers police not only the Capitol area, but the paranormal residents, too. *Photo by author*

is due to the fact there are people, potential witnesses, present within the haunted locations at all times of the day and even during the night. Without the presence of witnesses, how would ghostly activity ever be reported? And let's not dismiss the fact that the sheer nature of the job that the Capitol Police officers perform affords them more opportunity than the average person to experience paranormal activity—especially on the graveyard shift. Spending an entire midnight shift alone, locked within the walls of a haunted, historic building, could definitely be a formula for witnessing paranormal activity. And I'm willing to bet that people all over the world who perform functions similar to those of the officers of Virginia Capitol Police's graveyard shift, in equally historic locations, can likely recall similarly strange and exciting experiences.

Without a doubt, most of the buildings in and around the Capitol Complex possess a long and dramatic history. The Capitol Building, the Supreme Court, and the Governor's Mansion all experienced significant tragic events that could justify the level of paranormal energy within their walls. And this, I believe, is the number one reason why there appears to be such an exciting level of activity. With so much history, and of course tragedy, it is not difficult to believe that the restless spirits of the departed haunt the dark rooms and hallways of such old buildings. Coupled with the intense volume of living activity within the walls of the buildings on a daily and nightly basis, it is no wonder that both the living and the dead occasionally cross paths.

Surprisingly though, not all the buildings surrounding the Capitol have generated reports of haunting activity. From my own research, I have concluded that the General Assembly Building and Pocahontas Building, which both overlook portions of the Capitol Square and are both state-owned properties, lack any significant reports of ghostly phenomena. Having spent many graveyard shifts within the confines of both, I can personally attest to this fact. But, having both been constructed within the last fifty years, this seemingly lack of paranormal activity may support a theory that only the older buildings, which possess long, eventful, and often tragic histories, contain the mysterious elements necessary to produce paranormal activity. Who really knows?

As for the fact that certain people seem to witness ghostly activity while others don't, I personally believe that this phenomenon can easily be explained by the fact that some people are simply more observant than others. It's possible that some subtle paranormal activity simply goes unnoticed or ignored by potential witnesses, or the witnesses assume another more rational explanation. It may even be said that some people are more open-minded, or sensitive, to the presence of the supernatural, which makes them more susceptible to paranormal activity, causing them to perceive strange events in a different light. Even Mike Jones (retired Assistant Chief of Capitol Police) theorizes that if a person can "sense the deep history of a location," such as the Capitol and the Governor's Mansion, they may be far more sensitive to events and activity that may simply be ignored by others. But, regardless of their beliefs, while many witnesses appear adamant of their own level of skepticism, they also admit that they are without rational explanation for certain strange, personally observed, phenomena, adding credibility to the theory that alleged activity is not simply the result of overactive imaginations.

As I mentioned at the beginning of this book, I do not intend to convince people of the existence of ghosts in and around the buildings of Virginia's historic Capitol Complex. I simply wish to share with readers my experiences and the experiences of many others who have been privileged enough to have served with the Virginia Division of Capitol Police or have worked at many of the historic locations surrounding Capitol Square. I know for sure that there are many more witnesses to the ghostly goings-on in and around the State Capitol whom I have not interviewed, and there are also at least a couple more locations in close proximity to the Capitol where credible witnesses have reported experiencing strange phenomena. Unfortunately, due either to the fact that I was unable to interview the people or simply couldn't remember exactly who the people were who I had talked to when I was serving with the Virginia Capitol Police, I did not include the details of their experiences.

When discussing the Virginia Capitol Police and the officers who contributed their experiences to this book, I have to say that I do not doubt the credibility of any one of them. As a former Virginia Capitol Police officer and ten-year veteran of Virginia law enforcement, and having experienced some of the same eerie activity myself, I am confident of the credibility of the testimony of my colleagues. I have personally served alongside many of the officers who are mentioned in this book and have witnessed them keeping their cool during many high-stress situations. Therefore, I refuse to believe that such level-headed and rational individuals would suddenly resort to panic and illogical assumptions in the face of unexplained phenomena. Cops don't approach a situation with the idea that activity is paranormal. They first assume instinctively that activity is of a human criminal or mischievous nature and will investigate, evaluate, and report the facts, which is what I believe each officer has done when recalling their personal paranormal experiences. Also, most officers I worked alongside were genuine skeptics, until they experienced something that convinced them otherwise. Besides, none of the witnesses featured in this book were at any point purposely seeking out ghostly activity, and all reported phenomena were experienced unintentionally and without provocation in locations that are strongly considered to be haunted. I believe it is only after careful analysis of the particular activity and circumstances that most of the officers concluded that what they had witnessed was most likely paranormal.

Without conclusive evidence, such as that boasted by many paranormal TV shows, how will we ever know for sure? Maybe one day a team of paranormal experts will conduct an investigation around the Capitol Square, and maybe, just maybe, they will capture some sort of hard evidence that proves once and for all that ghosts really do exist within Virginia's historic Capitol Complex. I have to admit, I am surprised that there has never been an official investigation of the extraordinary activity conducted by a reputable paranormal investigation team within the aforementioned area. I can only assume that it's the previous lack of documented activity that has failed to attract such attention. Whatever the reason, wouldn't it be both interesting and fun to see one conducted?

I feel I must mention the fact that I am not exactly an avid fan of many of TV's ghost-hunting shows. Although I have a lot of respect for the actual investigators themselves, I believe that simply the fact that they are on TV doesn't afford them the opportunity to accurately portray to the viewers the lengthy amount of hours required to conduct a thorough investigation and capture some of the more compelling evidence. Viewers tend to think that the encounters occur regularly during the investigations, but it oftentimes takes much longer than TV can realistically depict while still providing an entertainment value.

On the other hand, I do enjoy reading about paranormal investigations conducted by reputable ghost hunters, and I certainly still enjoy watching the occasional ghost hunting related TV show as I find them entertaining and a great source of information on haunted locations throughout the world. On the topic of ghost investigators, I think any paranormal investigations group willing to conduct an official investigation, in what I and others consider quite possibly one of the most haunted locations in the U.S., would be absolutely amazed at the type of phenomena occurring so frequently in and around many of the buildings featured in this book.

On the topic of ghost investigations, one element of the haunting of the Capitol Complex that, in my opinion, places it above other alleged hauntings, in terms of quality and magnitude of the witnessed activity, is the occurrence of disembodied voices. Many professionally conducted ghost investigations, especially the TV shows, place a great deal of emphasis on the appeal of strange noises captured on electronic voice recorders. These strange noises often sound like faint voices, slightly audible within accompanying white noise, and are interpreted as *electronic voice phenomenon* (EVP). But although these EVP recordings are considered convincing evidence of the paranormal, most of them are only audible through electronic audio enhancement equipment. Considering that I and many other witnesses of the paranormal activity within the Capitol Complex not only heard faint voices, but entire conversations taking place within the confines of uninhabited and secure rooms, clearly audible without the use of electronic recording devices, I can only surmise that any paranormal investigator would find the Capitol's activity to be truly amazing; not to mention exciting and possibly downright scary! But I guess I'll leave that to the real ghost hunters.

While I and many other witnesses to unearthly activity believe in ghosts, I realize that I cannot convince every reader of this book of the existence of the paranormal. I only hope that everyone who does read this book does so with an open mind. As I have mentioned before, I am neither a ghost hunter nor a paranormal investigator, and I do not consider myself a psychic or sensitive. I am only fortunate enough to have experienced things that most people do not experience, as I frequently, yet unintentionally, crossed paths with the supernatural in places where most people do not get to venture. I also realize that there are those skeptics among us who will not believe the evidence unless a ghost appeared in front of them complete with rattling chains and piercing moans. What I would like readers to consider is that maybe, just maybe, there exists within our world another realm beyond logical and rational explanation, a realm that coexists and occasionally crosses paths with the living. It is these irregular and chance encounters between the living and the dead that have become locked within centuries of folklore, legends, and mystery and have become known throughout popular culture as ghost stories—tales that never fail to capture our imagination and thrill even the most skeptical among us.

So, if you are ever wondering what it is like to personally experience paranormal activity or what it may be like to conduct an investigation of your own, why not visit Virginia's historic State Capitol Complex? At the very least you could spend an entire day engulfed in the architectural splendor and political history of the location, or you may even meet one of the witnesses featured in this book. If you ever do visit the epicenter of Virginia politics, open your mind and try to imagine what it would be like to wander alone, during the midnight hours, within the rooms and corridors of each building, when everyone else has gone home and only strange shadows and faint whispers stir within the tranquil darkness of their walls.

I hope you enjoyed reading about the many encounters with the paranormal experienced by myself and others as we performed our daily duties. My only intent was to bring to light some of the astonishing paranormal activity frequently reported by citizens, employees, and police officers in and around Virginia's State Capitol. There are many books and articles in circulation that tell of ghosts and hauntings, but I believe none detail such a broad range of ghostly activity occurring within one particular location and reported by such a number of credible witnesses. I hope that readers won't only be entertained by the chilling details of many of the events, but by learning of the activity, will be motivated to explore the locations and the paranormal themselves. It's only through the knowledge and acceptance of the existence of ghosts that we can one day hope to understand and unlock the mysteries surrounding them. Regardless of any level of skepticism, as long as the subject of the paranormal continues to illicit excited fascination and intrigue, ghosts will always exist, even if only within the imaginations of those who truly believe.

Finally, if anyone who reads this book has had a ghostly experience in or around Virginia's Capitol Complex that they wish to share with others, please contact me at the listed email address. I may one day decide to write another exciting book containing more recent accounts of people's experiences with the ghosts that wander the same rooms and halls as our state legislators, for I, as well as many others, truly believe that the Capitol Police may not be the only force at work within the confines of Virginia's historic Capitol Square.

Sleep well!

Bibliography

Coakley, Frances. "A Manx Note Book: Inns of Douglas." http://www.isle-of-man.com/ manxnotebook/gazateer/inns/do_fl.htm#dhead/. 2001.

Darbyshire, Adrian. "Builders Uncover Woman's Skeleton at Nunnery." http://www. iomtoday.co.im/news/Builders-uncover-womans-skeleton-at.5336959.jp. June 6, 2009.

Executive Mansion (Virginia). http://en.wikipedia.org/wiki/Executive_Mansion_(Virginia). 2009.

Old City Hall (Richmond, Virginia). http://en.wikipedia.org/wiki/Old_City_Hall_(Richmond,_ Virginia). July, 11 2013.

Timeline of Events: In the History of the State Capitol Building and Square. http://www.vacapitol. org/timeline.htm. December 6, 2010.

Virginia State Capitol, About the Capitol: Capitol Square. http://www.virginiacapitol.gov/index. php?p=capitol_square. 2009.

Virginia's Executive Mansion: A Students Activity Book. (http://www.kidscommonwealth.virginia. gov/FunAndGames/ExecutiveMansionTeacherGuide.pdf)

Visitors and Newcomers: Old City Hall. RichmondGov.com. http://www.ci.richmond.va.us/ visitor/landmarks.aspx?flash=false. 2009.

Watson, Bill and Allen McCreary. "Gunfight in Basement." Richmond, VA: *The Richmond News Leader*, February 29, 1972.

Author Paul Hope standing atop Laxey Wheel, the world's largest working water wheel, overlooking the village of Laxey, Isle of Man.
Photo by Lisa Hope

About the Author

PAUL HOPE first experienced the paranormal during his childhood in the Isle of Man, British Isles. In 1996, at the age of 20, he emigrated to the United States, serving in the U.S. Army, and later, becoming a police officer in Virginia. It was as an officer that Paul once again encountered the paranormal while policing some of the most haunted and historical locations in the U.S.

Although having left law enforcement in late 2010 to pursue an opportunity as a private security contractor in Afghanistan, Paul continues to explore his lifelong interest in the supernatural. When not in Afghanistan, Paul lives on the outskirts of Richmond, Virginia, with his wife and daughter. He intends to eventually return to police work and his pursuit of the paranormal.